.

Don't Buy the Lie

Eradicating False Belief Systems
That Keep You From Your Destiny

Dr. Elizabeth D. Rios

Don't Buy the Lie © 2013
Dr. Elizabeth D. Rios

ISBN: 9780615748221

Library of Congress Control Number: 2012956462

Ghetto Rose Publications,
a division of the Center for Emerging Female Leadership
"Who said that a rose can't grow in the ghetto?"

Edited and Designed by RootSky Books
www.rootskybooks.com

First Edition

Printed and bound in the United States

"We cannot hold a torch to light another's path without brightening our own." — Ben Sweetland

To my husband Hiram thank you for being the torch that lit my path when my spark went out.

To my children Samuel Eliu and Daniel Jeremiah (DJ) you are my greatest legacy to the world

To those who have walked the path closely with me, thank you for seeing the me that was trying to emerge from beneath the rubble of broken dreams.

You all shine bright in my life.

Contents

Acknowledgments

I am so grateful to God that He saw fit to call me and give me the opportunity to educate, equip, empower, and inspire women, especially through my role as founder of the Center for Emerging Female Leadership (CEFL) and as a Pastor at Save the Nations Church. It is such an honor to speak into the lives of women. However, the things I do through CEFL as well as the writing of this book did not happen alone. I take this moment to acknowledge the people who have helped get this book into your hands.

I first acknowledge God who kept me — never would have made it without Him! Te Amo Senor con todo mi corazon!

To my amazing husband Hiram who loves me, supports me, and has kept his promise to always make me laugh and never to make me cry. Honey, your love and support are beyond astounding. When God created you he surely was thinking about me!

To my sons, Samuel Eliu and Daniel Jeremiah (DJ), I love you to the moon and back! Sam, I love the young man you are becoming. I'm so proud to be your mom and DJ, you've taught me more than most church sermons could. What a privilege God considered me the best mami for you!

To my mom, who as a single parent worked hard to give me the best she could afford. You instilled in me a love of books from an early age by taking me to the library!

To my WEPA girls past and present, Edna Quiros, Betsy Rivera, Marcy Ramos, Liz Martinez... your voices echo in my head many times, whether in laughter or in dispensing stories. I am a better person because you walked alongside me in my journey. I will never forget you. Ever.

To my Dream Team Group, Monica Carter Tagore at RootSky Books, Silvia Arvelo, Alba Arbelo, my incredible sister-in-love Enid Rios Rivera who always believed in the dream, my assistant and sister from another mister, Gladys

Rios... all of you played a role in getting this book out by giving me feedback, reading rough drafts, listening to my crazy thoughts and all the in-between support I could not have done without. Thank you for it all!

To my two church families, Primitive Christian Church in NYC and Save the Nations in Davie, Florida. Thank you to the lead pastors for believing in my gifting and allowing me to use it, whether in teaching, preaching, creating, or building. Thank you also to those members who supported me by attending my events and sending me encouraging email.

Preface

JANUARY 20, 2012

My life's mission as a pastor, educator, and women's empowerment coach has been to motivate people to change and to reach for their God-given dreams. This book is my heart on paper! I've lived this, and that is why I can write about it. My own belief systems (BS) prevented me from writing this book for so long. They told me I had so many reasons why I could never get this message out: I have so many roles. I am the mother of a special needs child. The time just wasn't right.

I originally began this book project on October 12, 2003, but I couldn't get it completed. Something seemed to always stand in the way. Again, the things that stood in the way were my belief systems, brought on by the lies of the devil. They urged me to push aside my dream. But I fought back against the negative messages floating around my head. I had a number of starts.

I finally made a determination that I had something to say that desperately needed to get in the hands of my sisters. And it wasn't going to write itself.

Along the way, I found a book agent who was interested in the project, but since it took so long for me to complete, my agent disappeared. Again, something seemed to be standing in the way.

My belief systems could have held me hostage, convincing me that the lost opportunity meant my book would never get in front of the sisters who needed it. I could have let that delay me yet again because now I didn't have someone going to bat for me with publishing companies.

But that's not what happened.

I refused to let my belief systems — brought on by the lies of the enemy — keep me from my God-appointed destiny.

I knew in my heart that there are many women like me who think because of the way life has turned out that they can't possibly do something great. That's another lie of the enemy.

I was sitting in a hospital room in Florida after the near loss of my son, Daniel Jeremiah on Mother's Day 2007. Emotionally drained and physically exhausted, my mind went to this book. *I have to finish my book!* The thought hit me with force.

On that day he was resuscitated five times. God allowed him to come back to me because it just was not time for him to die. I cried a lot on that Mother's Day because I was preparing for loss and yet another scar. God spared me from that one. However, while I sat in the hospital, so thankful to have my son, my mind also went to a place where I thought about you, because in a very real way, what happened to my son happens to countless people around the world every day. You come close to dying.

Or maybe some of you — if you dare to admit it — are already dead inside. The life line of your dreams has slowly faded away and you just don't have the energy to find the instrument you need to resuscitate it.

That's how this book came to be. It was a struggle and a major fight against my belief systems. But I fought back and overcame those crippling ideas.

As I write this book to you today, I am thankful for the journey. My belief systems tried to hold me back, but God blessed me to see through the devil's lies.

I now share this message with you.

Your Sister, Tu Hermana

Elizabeth D. Rios

Introduction

Maybe you have been coasting through life for way too long. It seems that it's your time — and your time AGAIN! You keep seeing opportunities, but you never quite take them. Something holds you back. How many years have already passed you by? What have you been waiting for? If you're like I was for a long time, you're not even sure of what's holding you back.

You think it's your work schedule. The fact that your family keeps you busy. The fact that you have way too many demands.

But that's not it.

It's something much deeper than that.

That's the purpose of this book. It's to share with you the real reason your life might not be going as you want. The real reason it seems that countless opportunities have passed you by. The real reason you just can't seem to be as bold as you know God wants you to be.

Maybe you are looking for some perspective, or you want to believe there is hope for you. You've had a lot of rough patches in your life, it's almost felt like a rainfall of hardship and you really want to learn how to live the life God wants you live, that life you heard about that is an abundant, joyful life. You want to hear **how** you can get up, stay up and start moving in the direction of your dreams and God's destiny for you.

How... is important because most of us believe God can help us — we just don't know **how** we can cooperate with Him to get us in position to live life on purpose! Right?! Well that is my drive for writing this book, I want to just take off the mask and share with you my story. Perhaps as I share my story, *you will find your story.* A story of how you have had to struggle most of your life. A story of how nothing has been handed to you. A story of how many times in life as the

Word tells us, you just have to "encourage yourself!"

My story is about how a limitless God can take a girl from a single-parent home in the projects of Avenue D (read *ghetto,* before gentrification took over) in New York City's tough Lower East Side and use her life and her words to become a recognized writer, ministry leader, and respected educator. How this tough Lower East Side girl grew up in church but didn't really grow up in God until crisis hit her life in ways she would have never dreamed. Bottom line, I want to share with you some B.S. that helped me get through all the trials and valleys of my life. Thanks to the lies of the enemy, all of us carry B.S. around — some of us are just not aware of it!

We are full of more BS than you would imagine.

BS doesn't always have to be negative. BS can actually be good for you, if of course, you are full of the right kind! In case you are already ready to put down this book because it is way too "liberal" for a Christian book, let me just calm you down right now... BS is Belief Systems!

Now it is this very BS that can either help you get up and keep walking or stay down, roll over and play dead. The way you change your life is to change your mindset about how you deal with the challenges of life. You have to trade bad (ungodly) BS with good (Godly) BS. The ungodly BS is the stuff that holds us back, and it's all anchored to lies that have seeped into our minds.

I've battled bad BS and have worked hard — at times, struggled — to overcome and replace them with good BS.

God has given me an amazing understanding of the BS that holds us back, and I hope your eyes are opened as you read the next few pages.

So come on, let's get over the BS and lies.

CHAPTER 1

LIAR, LIAR, PANTS ON FIRE

This chapter's title is the basic truth and essence of this book. You may have heard it as a chant normally used by children to indicate they think someone is lying. It's actually a paraphrase from an 1810 poem by William Blake titled "The Liar." While its origin is not relevant to the purpose of this book, its message is. Someone has been lying to you since you could discern voice. That someone is known to believers as Satan and as the scripture verse reminds us, he is the father of lies. He's the one we have to chant back to when we hear his voice telling us something contrary to what God says about us!

For most of my life, I believed many of the lies he whispered to me. For a better part of my life, I also didn't attempt great things for God because I simply believed that God was not on MY side. The devil did a good job making me believe that the direction of my life was already set and I bought it...for a time. Thankfully one day I woke up and now I want to share what I view is the basic message of my life. You can get up from ANYTHING. You can achieve anything you put your mind to if God called you to it, IF you don't buy the lie.

The lies you believe keep you from what God has for you. There are lies we buy about Satan, there are lies we buy about God, and there are lies we buy about ourselves. All the lies are obstacles to us getting everything God destined for us because they keep us believing something that is not true.

For example, if we believe that no one can ever love us, we settle for relationships that are less than God's best for us — many times outright abusive relationships —simply because we believe that's the best we can do. We'd rather settle for bad than believe for best.

That's Satan's power of deception. This is his tool. He lies to us mainly in three areas as we make perverted attempts to satisfy three desires: the attempt to satisfy physical needs, the attempt to satisfy personal gain, or the attempt to attain power and glory. God has already given us truth in these three areas, but it is Satan's goal to convince us that God's Word is not as important as our fallen human nature and desire.

WHO IS THIS LIAR?

The liar known as Satan means "adversary." Satan is the enemy of God. He wants to destroy everything God has created and by default anyone who seeks to follow God. He is also called "the devil" (James 4:7), "the evil one" (1 John 5:18-19), "the prince of this world" (John 14:30), and "the god of this age" (2 Corinthians 4:4). Satan brought evil into the world and he wants to destroy every good thing God destined to come to you and through you!

He's been lying to us since the beginning of creation and yes, we bought the lie and because of it sin entered this world. Yet, we don't have to continue to buy the lie! As we get wise to the schemes of the enemy and know the tactics that he uses to get us to buy his deception, we won't be taken advantage of due to lack of knowledge.

The Word reminds us in 2 Corinthians 2:11: "In order that no advantage be taken of us by Satan; for we are not ignorant of his (Satan's) schemes." Ephesians 6:10-12: "Finally, be strong in the Lord, and in the strength of His might. Put on the full armor of God, that you may be able to stand firm against the schemes of the devil. For our struggle is not against flesh and blood, but against the rulers, against the powers, against the world forces of this darkness, against the spiritual forces of wickedness in the heavenly places."

Satan has a plan, and so you must have a plan, too. If not, you will (and probably already have) been eaten alive — spiritually, that is.

Why do we keep falling for his lies? I came to the conclusion that it is because we love a good preacher!

SATAN IS A GOOD PREACHER

From the third chapter of the Bible onward, he is opening up God's Word to people, seeking to interpret it, to apply it, to offer an invitation. So the old Serpent of Eden comes to the primeval woman not with a Black Mass and occult symbols, but with the Word she'd received from her God — with the snake's peculiar spin on it. Throughout the rest of the history he does the same, implicitly or explicitly. He's the original spin master!

Let's take a look, shall we? Throughout the Old Testament, he preaches peace — just like the angels of Bethlehem do — except he does so when there is no peace. He points God's people to the particulars of worship commanded by God — sacrifices and offerings and feast-days — just without the preeminent mandates of love, justice, and mercy. Satan even preaches to God — about the proper motives needed for godly discipleship on the part of God's servants.

In the New Testament, the satanic deception leads the scribes, Pharisees, and Sadducees to pore endlessly over biblical texts, just missing the point of Jesus's purpose on earth. They come to conclusions that have partially biblical foundations — the devil's messages are always expository; they just intentionally avoid Jesus.

So, the scoffers feel quite comfortable asking how a man from Nazareth could be the Messiah when the coming King is of Bethlehem. They find themselves wondering how the Son of Man can be crucified when the Bible says he lives forever. When Jesus says those who follow him should eat his flesh and drink his blood, there's little doubt that the Adversary was there to point the crowds to Leviticus's forbidding of the consumption of human blood. When the satanically inspired crowds crucified Jesus, they did so pointing to biblical texts that called for the execution of blasphemers and insurrectionists (Deut. 21).

When the early church rockets out of the upper room in Jerusalem, *Satan is there*, with false teachers, to preach all kinds of things that *seem* to be straight from God's Word — from libertinism to legalism to hyper-spirituality to carnality. He never stops preaching and for the most part, most people never stop buying his lies!

HE LIES IN BIG AND LITTLE THINGS

The devil is a liar! For real. It's not just a church insider joke. He's a liar but he is not to blame for everything, although I know he should get at least partial credit for some. It's him whispering into the ears of some people to make them do things. Folks have just got to figure out when not to listen to that lying little voice at times. The devil does lie and I know people who believed him:

• To the lady with 20 extra pounds right around her middle. The devil lied when he said you'd look good wearing the low-rise jeans with the high-rise top.

• To anyone older than 25, the devil lied when he said you would look cute with Kool-Aid-colored hair cut into a funky style.

• To anyone who confuses being "real" with a license to be rude, the devil lied when he said you could treat people any way you please. Rudeness is not cute. You don't have to smile to make my day, but walking around looking like we all ticked you off does not help you along in life.

• To any young person who insists on cussing and acting thuggish, the devil lied when he said it would make you look grown. It makes you look unemployable and worrisome. It either frightens or disgusts the rest of us.

• To married people who quit trying, the devil lied when he told you courtship ends at the altar. Work at your marriage and stop blaming the devil. You bought the lie AND drank the Kool-Aid.

• To Christians, the devil lied when he said it's your duty to judge everyone who crosses your path. You are not the Lord; you are His children and the "sinners" of the world are your brothers and sisters. I think God wants us to love our family. Love does not equal agreement on everything, but it still means LOVE. (And, by the way, your sins of lying or greed are no less or greater in God's eyes than someone else's sexual sins or sins of murder.)

• To non-Christians, the devil lied when he told you that one bad experience with a Christian meant all Christians are that way. Some Christians get the "love" thing, so don't judge all Christians because of some bad Christians in your life.

So you see, what I mean. The devil does not want us to recognize truth — in big things or in little things. A lie is a lie is a lie.

THE BOTTOM LINE — SATAN IS OUT TO DESTROY YOU!

He will do it with his lies. This is no scare tactic. The kingdom of darkness seeks to rule our world today. It is as real as light and darkness. The spiritual blindness Satan seeks to instill into our hearts is designed to make our world a dark place to live. The darkness Satan seeks to impose upon our world is designed to lead us to a point where every thought and inclination of our hearts is evil continually. Don't forget, he has done it once and he seeks to do it again (Genesis 6:5). In the following verse Paul describes such a world.

Ephesians 4:18-19 (NIV): "They are darkened in their understanding and separated from the life of God because of the ignorance that is in them due to the hardening of their hearts. Having lost all sensitivity, they have given themselves over to sensuality so as to indulge in every kind of impurity, with a continual lust for more."

Doesn't this sound a lot like the world we live in right now?

I once heard a story about ants that I think makes for a great illustration of what Satan sets out to do:

In the jungles of the Amazon there is a slave-making ant that's really just like the devil. Hundreds of these ants of the Amazon periodically swarm out of their nest to capture neighboring colonies of weaker ants. After destroying resisting defenders, they carry off cocoons containing the larvae of worker ants. When these "captured children" hatch, they assume that they are part of the family and launch into the tasks they were born to do. They never realize that they are forced-labor victims of the enemy. Just as these little creatures are bound from the time of their birth, so we enter the world enslaved to sin and Satan.

The deceitfulness of Satan's tactics blinds us to his enslavement. It blinds us to the ferocious battle he is actually fighting to gain control of our world and our individual destinies.

He's the liar I want to remind you about to help you eradicate the lies you have already bought into. I want to get you out of the captivity mentality that keeps you doing things you think you were "born into" like those ants and help you determine in your heart that you will never again buy one of his lies!

THE MURDERING LIAR

I end with how I started, the devil is a liar. Period. (Punto). Caso cerrado! (Case closed). "You belong to your father the devil, and you want to do what he wants. He was a murderer from the beginning and was against the truth, because there is no truth in him. When he tells a lie, he shows what he is really like, because he is a liar and the father of lies." John 8:44 NCV

His world is a world of lies. When Jesus says there is no truth in Satan, he is telling us quite a bit. He's out for all that you are, all that you represent. He's out to kill you and thus your impact in the kingdom on the lives of others. Remember, the devil will always do that through lies. He did it with Eve, he worked on Jesus the same way, and we too can expect him to approach us with his most powerful weapon: the lie.

Your destiny is tied to what you believe from here on out. Next up: Learning when you bought the lie.

EXERCISE: Think about three negative beliefs you have. Write about them here. We will discuss them later.

_____

_____

_____

CHAPTER 2

WHY DO WE BUY THE LIE?

Definition of Core Beliefs: *Basic underlying imprint you subconsciously hold to be true about yourself*

What you believe is *the* crucial aspect that determines your entire experience of life! That's right. Beliefs are so important, yet most of us have given this very little brain time. No wonder so many people never reach their God-given destiny! Simply put, we buy the lie because we believe something about ourselves that is not in line with what God says about us and our future. It's basically an ungodly belief!

Core beliefs are those things you just know and trust to be true — they serve as an internal *guide to life*, telling you how to behave and react to the world. Yet core beliefs were only meant to be temporary — to be used until we were mature enough to take charge of our own life.

The good news is that when you release a core belief by understanding and believing God's Word, a *Core Truth* automatically comes to replace it. You will discover that everyone, to some extent, contains, in their belief system (BS), beliefs that are not true. When these beliefs are contrary to what God's Word says, we call those "ungodly." That means there is a lot of bad BS in our minds! This type of BS is very dangerous and let me tell you why... it guides our decision-making because it affects our perceptions, our decisions, and our actions. This affects our destiny and that's why this type of BS must be dealt with if you ever expect to be who God created you to be and do what He created you to do. Do you get the urgency here? Some people die never having addressed their BS — with potential still inside. Don't let that be YOU! There is a poem I came across years ago and perhaps you have seen it too, by an unknown author that I believe illustrates the progression of BS in a powerful way.

Belief System
If you accept a Belief, you reap a Thought.
If you sow a Thought, you reap an Attitude.
If you sow an Attitude, you reap an Action.
If you sow an Action, you reap a Habit.
If you sow a Habit, you reap a Character.
If you sow a Character, you reap a Destiny.

Do you see that? It starts with a seed of belief and ends up messing with your destiny! Godly beliefs, godly destiny, and the opposite is true as well! The realization that what you've been living and telling yourself all these years was based on a skewed perception of something that happened as a child, is a freeing moment. You have to wonder how you didn't figure it out a long time ago. The truth is that the church doesn't really talk about these things because for many, it is not "spiritual" enough to address from the pulpit. Thankfully pastors like Pete Scazzero and others have addressed emotionally healthy spirituality and practices like spiritual direction have helped many get in touch with God's voice and reflect on when debilitating, ungodly beliefs were introduced to us.

I wrote this book because I have lived on both sides of this belief fence. I used to believe I wasn't good enough because of mistakes I made in my past and unfortunately some people in the faith community perpetuated that core belief. That wasn't helpful! But as I grew up and surrounded myself with people who were on the same journey, I learned that I had been filled with garbage. And like the old computer saying goes, "garbage in, garbage out," I had my aha moment in my mid-30s, after a crash into Calvary moment! Some people never get that moment because they are not exposed to the information and don't seek it out either. Yet this is literally so important, God did not let me wimp out of writing this book.

You see, your core beliefs dictate the life you live. They show up in:
• Who you are
• What you think of yourself
• What you are and are not allowed to do and be
• How you behave and react to people, experiences, and the world
• What you expect
• Your success
• What you think you can and cannot have

So let me make sure you now understand the difference between BS that is ungodly versus godly.

Ungodly beliefs: all beliefs, decisions, attitudes, agreements, judgments, expectations, vows, and oaths that **do not** agree with God's Word about His nature or character.

Godly beliefs: all beliefs, decisions, attitudes, agreements, judgments, expectations, vows, and oaths that **do** agree with God's Word about His nature or character.

Understanding these types of BS helps us to understand why we have been buying the lies of the enemy for so long! We've been living with ungodly BS! How do you know? You will know because a real godly belief will be reflected in your actions, will be rooted in your heart, and will stand firm in the heat of battle with the enemy's whispers.

HOW WE DEVELOP BELIEF SYSTEMS

From the moment you come into the world, you begin developing your belief system. Your system of beliefs forms from irrational input as well as rational! You don't have a filter or flag that lets you know the difference.

Obviously as a newborn you don't have a well-formed capacity for logical deduction, so developing your belief system is not necessarily a rational process. Rather, it's a process based on your experience of the world.

Whatever information comes to you in a form that you can digest, (i.e. you have the necessary perception to process it), you file appropriately into your fledgling belief system.

As you mature, your abilities and understanding expands, and ultimately you are developing your belief system based on five primary methods of gathering information. Only one of these stems directly from your personal facility of critical thinking!

It can be very helpful and enlightening to know why you believe what you do. You might be surprised to realize some of the shaky ground you have formed your belief system on.

The big five BS feeders are:

1. Evidence
2. Tradition
3. Authority
4. Association
5. Revelation

EVIDENCE-BASED BELIEVING

Evidence shows that one thing causes another. The understanding of relationship appeals to the analytical and critical thinking part of your mind. Developing your belief system through this method is very rational and based on the use of logical thinking.

The skills associated with evidence-based believing develop as we mature, and become more honed through education. In this method you look for facts. You look at events that are measurable, and where one thing directly causes something else.

You can also establish beliefs based on your personal experience of cause and effect. You might continually witness a consistent outcome from your actions. For example:

• If you drive a certain route at rush hour, you know you will be 10 minutes late and upset yourself and others. Therefore you believe it's best to take an alternate route during rush hour.

• When you make dinner for friends, they express their appreciation, and you feel great. Therefore you know you will get enjoyment by creating dinner for friends.

This method of forming beliefs is also responsible for "learned helplessness." If you consistently perform a behavior, and always get a negative outcome, you may come to believe that you have no power or influence in creating what it is you are aiming for. For example:

• Because you are always 10 minutes late when driving that certain route at rush hour, and it is the only route possible to take, you know you will be 10 minutes late. You will feel upset, and you will upset others. Therefore, you always feel distressed in this situation.

• When you make dinner for friends, no one expresses their appreciation, and you feel like a failure. Therefore you stop cooking dinner for friends.

The trick in the learned helplessness scenario is to adjust the elements that you can, and accept the things you cannot change. This might possibly include altering the physical elements such as setting alternate meeting times or places, or cooking different meals or inviting different friends!

But certainly one thing you can change, through gaining understanding, is how you view these events. For example, you could say:

• If that is the only route possible to take during rush hour, and I cannot change appointment details or start the drive 10 minutes early, I will be 10 minutes late. That is reality.

Therefore, I have 10 minutes in traffic to put to use as I wish by listening to relaxing radio, personal development recordings, or reviewing the things I'm thankful for today. I will explain this situation to any other people affected.

Whether they decide to make the best of the situation, is up to them. I am not responsible for how they view reality.

• If I cook dinner for friends, and no one expresses appreciation, I can ask myself exactly why it is that I want to cook these dinners.

•

If you feel like a failure when no one expresses appreciation, then you are likely looking to others to reinforce your self-worth. That shows it's time to recognize that your self-worth is something always with you. To tap into it, spend some time talking to a life coach for personal development.

ADOPTING TRADITIONAL BELIEFS

The traditions perpetuated through families and societies are a major factor in developing your belief system. We are often showered with traditions day in and day out when growing up, so they can be extremely easy to adopt, without even questioning. When you believe in traditions, recognize that they have served some generation well. Yet it does not mean they are based in truth, nor necessarily have continued usefulness for your life.

There is a funny and telling story about a woman from a certain family where the women always cut their roasts in half prior to roasting. The third-generation daughter said she did it because she understood that it made the meat tender. Her mother said that she learned it from her own mom and thought it was to reduce the cooking time and save on energy usage. When the oldest woman, Grandma, was asked about it, she said that the oven she had when raising a family was very small and it was necessary to always cut the roast in half to fit it in!

So not only was there a belief being passed down that it was important to cut the roast in half, the reason behind the belief was totally lost, and no longer relevant to the women's lives!

In my own life I remember my grandmother telling me that I could get pregnant if I had a bathing suit on and a boy kissed me. Needless to say, for many, many years I did not let a boy kiss me with a bathing suit on! The things mothers and grandmothers do to keep their daughters and granddaughters from close contact with the opposite sex!

Another belief system I got from my mother was that all men are pigs and that I should never depend on one. Thus, my mandate was to get an education so if the one I ended up marrying "walked out on me" I would be able to support myself. Of course, I eventually learned that not "all" men are pigs and that some are trustworthy but I had to learn that on my own with my own journey with men.

So, it is through family and cultural traditions that many people formulate their primary belief system. Social culture, family bias, and societal prejudice all strongly influence formation of:

Global beliefs such as:
• what God is
• political theory
• science
• personal value

Topic-specific beliefs:
• the specific religious practice to support
• which political party to vote for
• which sport team to cheer for

Tradition and our attention to the past can actually prevent us from seeing what is right in front of us, in the present, according to Jiddu Krishnamurti.[1]

Ask yourself what role tradition has played in developing your belief system.

---

[1] Jiddu Krishnamurti. The Awakening of Intelligence. Harper & Row. 1987.

AUTHORITY STEERS BELIEFS

Many beliefs are adopted from people who have roles of authority in our lives. Sometimes these figures of authority also fall into the category of tradition, as you can imagine. For example, your parents play a role of authority in your early life and they are regularly passing traditions down to you.

Other times authority figures are independent of tradition. Some examples of authority figures who may influence your beliefs, while theirs are not necessarily based on traditional beliefs, might be:

• a religious leader that espouses having a special direct line to God

• doctors who tell you they absolutely know best about your health and all conflicting ideas are rubbish

• a school teacher you look up to, whether or not he or she follows "tradition"

This is probably one of the biggest ways our belief system is formed. We see this especially in the case of religious leaders. It's amazing how many Christians believe what their pastor tells them and accept it as gospel because they never picked up the Word of God and learned for themselves what God's promises are for them and how He wants them to run their lives.

It reminds me of the day the pastor of my New York home church (when I was about 15) told my mom that a hickey I had received from my then-boyfriend was the mark of a prostitute and she believed him! His authority as pastor poisoned my mom's thinking of me as a teen and it was something I had to live through that I will never forget.

BELIEFS BY ASSOCIATION

With whom do you hang out? Whether you run with the "in crowd" or the "nerds," you will be adopting compatible beliefs to your own, as well as reinforcing common beliefs that you hold with your group. It is pretty much a case of "what you see is what you get." As you are continually faced with particular ways of thinking within the group, you start to adopt and reinforce those ideas as the "right way" to think.

Basically, by sharing time and activities, you rub off on one another and mutually influence one another's belief system. If you associate with hard working people who feel they are short on time and money, chances are you will be developing your belief system based around those ideas as well.

Alternatively, if you spend your time with people who feel they have a very rich, blessed life spending their time for their own delight, your attitude will likely be quite different.

I'm non-apologetic about with whom I spend my very limited time. As a pastor, that gets me in trouble sometimes because some people feel I should hang out with everyone, accept every invitation, and just play nice. But I have learned the importance of whom you hang out with because they have the power to poison your well and I need my well pure in belief so I can dispense it to others.

REVELATIONS INDUCE BELIEFS

Revelation is when we receive truth from the supernatural. Basically, this is the experience of attaining information through what you might describe as:
• a feeling or sense about something
• a hunch or an inkling of an idea
• an intuition or premonition about something

• a gut feeling
• your imagination
• something you believe to be God

Most beliefs you hold have not originated with you. Rather, you have primarily adopted what makes sense to your experience and understanding at the time. You continue in developing your belief system largely by agreeing with ideas that come into your awareness.

Once you understand this, it gives you great strength to:

• Review your beliefs, and ask with non-attachment, "Do they have a solid basis and do they serve me well?"

• Drop any feeling of threat when your adopted beliefs seem to fall short, or come under attack. You have accepted your beliefs based on what you knew at the time. As you learn more, it is reasonable that your belief system will undergo change and growth. That's my hope for you after you read this book!

We see the world around us and our place in it from the perspective of our personal belief systems. Whether we ascribe to a particular faith tradition or not, we have values based on the beliefs that we hold to be true. Belief systems change over time — adjusting to the ebb and flow of life experience and growing with maturity and formation in our faith tradition. Throughout our entire life, the struggle to make sense of our existence is played out in our interior conflicts between faith and disbelief.

The realm of disbelief opens up like a sea of uncertainty. "But when you ask, you must believe and not doubt, because the one who doubts is like a wave of the sea, blown and tossed by the wind." (James 1:6 TNIV) The questioning of one belief calls another into question and so on until the whole set of beliefs is tossed in turmoil.

The voice of our conscience may call us to come back to our senses, but to listen to that interior voice takes an act of will. "Cling to your faith in Christ, and keep your conscience clear. For some people have deliberately violated their consciences; as a result, their faith has been shipwrecked." (1 Timothy 1:19 NLT)

Whether out of weakness, distress, or a conscious decision, to surrender to disbelief is to abandon one's faith. The decision to have faith is an act of will which strengthens our resolve in the face of uncertainty.

Hannah was a woman in the Bible who showed unbelievable faith in the face of uncertainty.[2] She was barren and as such, had to face the ridicule of those around her. Her husband's other wife, Peninnah, had children and liked to make fun of Hannah because of Hannah's lack of children. Sometimes, the insults hurt so much that Hannah broke down in tears.

On one such occasion, Hannah went to the house of the Lord, pouring out her heart to Him and praying for a child.

The priest saw her and at first thought she was drunk, but upon speaking with her realized she was simply begging God for a miracle. The priest, Eli, encouraged her that she might get her miracle and she left there, happy and no longer upset.

In due time, Hannah became pregnant and fulfilled her promise to God — she dedicated her son Samuel to the Lord.

I love this story of Hannah because it reminds me so much of our modern-day world. Hannah had to face the ridicule of a fellow woman and a member of her own family, but that negativity didn't cause Hannah to turn away from faith. Instead, she prayed even harder.

You see, people may make fun of you and even try to make you feel bad about yourself, but if you hold onto your faith — even in the face of uncertainty — you too can prevail.

---

[2] 1 Samuel 1.

GOING BACK TO CHILDHOOD

Because a child's role is to learn how to live as a human being, we used all that we saw, heard, and experienced to form a set of core beliefs about who and what we are, the world and our place in it. These beliefs were not chosen, but instead reflect the *conclusions* that you and I reached about our particular experiences from our limited perception.

Your core beliefs are *neither* dysfunctional nor lopsided. They are valid conclusions that were reached **by a child**, from that child's current perception of an experience *at that time*. It is, however, inappropriate and often dysfunctional to filter your entire adult experience according to the life rules of a child, especially if you have been hearing and reading the Word of God. Something is not sticking!

Every family has problems, as there is no perfect parent. Therefore, all children develop mistaken core beliefs about themselves, the world, and their place in it. A practical example of this idea might be how you interpret and integrate an experience like the divorce of your parents. This event may lead you to conclude *"it is my fault,"* therefore create the belief, *"I am a bad person and do not deserve good things."* You may develop a tendency to punish yourself and sabotage your success without any idea that you are doing so.

Naturally, the people who endure horrific life experiences (neglect, abuse, assault, death of a loved one, betrayal, and natural disasters, for example) often form harsh conclusions (core beliefs) to base their self-concepts and life on. These conclusions, along with the expected emotional responses and the shock of having had this experience are stored in the subconscious. In effect, their entire perception of life is based on those tragic events.

I myself had developed deeply ingrained core beliefs due to the fact that my father left my home when I was two years old. I grew up with a single mom. Since my family always struggled for "things" money could buy, I thought being poor was the norm and that God must not have loved me like others because he allowed all that to happen. Remember the hickey incident I hinted at earlier? This is what went down, and how it formed a belief system that stayed with me for years:

I was in my teens when my first negative belief system *that I recall* about church was formed. I was 15 when the boyfriend I had at the time gave me a hickey. I grew up in a Spanish-speaking legalistic Assembly of God church and dating at that time constituted sending each other notes in between prayers while the girls and boys sat on opposite sides of the church. I really didn't even know what a hickey was other than it was a red mark on the neck — a mark my mother had shown me in a picture of my cousin a while back, one that he had sent us for a Christmas greeting and of which she mentioned, "never get one of *those*," as she pointed to the red mark.

I filed that away in the recesses of my memory bank and it only returned suddenly when I was facing the mirror staring at the mark on my neck! Who knew someone nibbling at my neck would cause the "the mark?" Unfortunately, I would find out the hard way.

Quickly thinking of a way out of the situation so my mom wouldn't find out and beat the living day lights out of me, I planned what I thought was a great strategy. The next day I was leaving to visit my aunt in Boston. By the time I would be back the mark would surely be gone. Master plan, right?

But it didn't work out that way. Right after our Sunday school session, someone called out my name and I turned my neck (which was nicely covered by my lifted collar — we were in the Fonzie era, don't judge me). My mom caught a glance at it and pulled my collar down and discovered "the mark." Not only did she slap me right there, in front of the entire church (embarrassed doesn't even cover what I felt), but then she said we were going to have a meeting at home with my uncle Johnny (the male father figure who also was a deacon of the church) and my aunt, his wife.

When I got home I wanted to just die, so I did the next best thing I could think of at the time: I went to take a nap. Something about naps helps you block out the world. I guess that's why I still take them. My mom, a new convert from Catholicism a year back, was crying. She wanted to know what was the "procedure" for something like this. Well, my uncle said the pastor needed to know. (At that time, church folk — especially Latino church folk — told the pastors everything, and I mean everything.) They would meet with the pastor right before the night service. They woke me up to tell me this exciting news. I was thrilled, as you might imagine. I could literally feel the minutes passing by as we waited to have the sit-down with the pastor.

What happened next marked me for life and formed BS that I would carry for a long, long time. We arrived at church. The pastor's office was in the basement and covered in lovely brown wood paneling, did you catch that sarcasm? I could see the disdain in his eyes. My heart is racing. Especially because I just passed a few hermanas I knew were making me the topic of their pre-prayer time discussion before the service started.

The pastor proceeded to ask my mother questions about what bought her to his office and then after hearing the story — her story — told my mother his brilliant response. He said, wait for it, wait for it... he said that a *hickey was the sign of a prostitute.*

A prostitute? I was a virgin.

My mother cried. To this day I don't even know what she was thinking, but obviously it was not good. What mom wants to hear that her daughter has a mark of a prostitute?

As we went upstairs for service, I was told to sit in the back. At that time, in the mid 70's, the back of the church was a sign of "the unwanted, the sinful, the rejects, the outcasts."

The service went on and when the time for the program came, the pastor dutifully (joyfully) announced to the *entire* congregation yes *everyone* present at that service, that I along with my male friend would be on "discipline," a type of punishment for whatever duration of time they pronounced (for me it was six months) you were not allowed to attend any church events, socialize with any church members or take part in any ministry you may have been part of. When the pastor announced my name, the entire church looked back (okay maybe not the *entire* church, but it sure seemed like it).

From that day on, some mothers would tell their daughters not to hang out with me; they would tell their sons that I was not a "good girl," certainly not one that they would want them to bring home for any serious relationship — of course, many were in denial themselves about their own children who were smoking, drinking, getting hickeys of their own (in places where *the sun don't shine* as one pastor's daughter told me I should have done it) and in some cases already sexually active. I guess talking about the girl "who got caught" was better than facing their own situations. But it formed the following BS in me that made me buy these lies:

1) Church people don't really care.

2) Church people won't be there for you when you really need them.

3) Church people can't and should never be trusted.

4) Church people do what they tell you not to do. They just learn not to get caught.

5) God must have been out on vacation when that was all going down.

You live what you believe. And I lived it for the longest. I rejected church people, their promises, and their associations.

•

Every person lives the core beliefs that they formed as a child. It is impossible to live anything else as they are your rules of life — *your truth*. This is what I am trying to combat in this book. Your truth may be valid in the sense that you experienced what you experienced but that doesn't negate the fact that God's truth overrules your truth and that our process in becoming healthy disciples on our way to the destiny God has for us involves making His truths our truths.

•

I have a confession. As a result of the core beliefs formed when I was a child, for most of my life, I felt like God's stepchild, not his favorite child as Mikel French, an evangelist I met, likes to say in his preaching! I felt overlooked, slightly loved, and partially nurtured by family as well as the church.

My old belief system caused me a lot of pain.

EXERCISE: Go back to the negative beliefs you wrote about in the previous chapter. Now, think back to when you formed them. Write about that here. Use more paper or a notebook, if necessary. What was going on? What made you think these beliefs were true?

_____

_____

_____

CHAPTER 3

THE ENEMY USES BS TO MAKE US BELIEVE HIS LIES

I began going to church when I was 10 years old. Prior to that, I was Catholic like most Latinos in America. Sunday Mass attending yet non-practicing Catholic. My uncle Johnny Rosa has a reward in heaven for being the male father figure in my life and introducing me to Christianity at this age. My father who, was a preacher at night but a drunkard and wife abuser by day, left my mom with me when I was just two years old. My mom came home to an empty apartment at 268 Stagg Street in Williamsburg, Brooklyn. She had to begin again alone and to this day, I've never met my father. What an awesome daughter he missed out on!

I formed certain belief systems about men, relationships, and my lovability, based on my father's absence and the life my mother and I had. As I mentioned earlier, belief systems are formed throughout life, but especially during the time from birth through early childhood. Our core beliefs around love and security are usually formed by the time we are four years old because those two areas are necessary for survival. If we aren't loved and cared for enough or aren't safe, then we instinctively know we can die. While you may believe, and have experienced, that your parents didn't love you or you weren't safe, the fact that you are alive shows that you had enough love and security to survive.

This is how a belief system is formed. Let's say you're a one-year-old and standing in your crib and crying to be picked up. This is a common experience all children have. However, it may be that this time you cry too long and decide that no one is coming to pick you up because you're not lovable. If you were lovable, or good enough, then someone would be there for you. Since your mother doesn't come for you, then that proves there's something wrong with you. None of this is logical thinking, or in any way conscious, yet it occurs in all of us over and over again.

•

In that moment of stress and despair, a belief system is

formed and encompasses four elements: (1) your thought of "I'm not good enough," (2) your emotions in the crib, (3) your age of one, and (4) the event of no one coming to pick you up. All four elements become locked together and programmed into your subconscious mind as *"this is what's true about me."* From then on, that thought can become reinforced and more real for you as life goes on. As a teenager, you may not get picked for a team. During dating, the person you are crazy about likes someone else. In your job, you get passed over for promotions. As life's events happen, they are filtered through this belief and you respond with *"See, more proof, I'm not good enough."*

Let me give you another example. A thirsty 4-year-old child is reaching for her drink, which is up on a counter. She struggles to reach it but can't, and nobody comes to help her. So she sits down on the floor and feels overwhelmed and helpless. She turns her attention inside to console herself. In that moment, a belief is formed, which if it isn't changed or updated, can cause her to close down and feel helpless or overwhelmed as an adult when she can't see a solution. In reality, there was a kitchen chair available that the child could have pulled over and stood on to reach her drink. It may even be that a few minutes later she saw the chair, retrieved her drink, and went on her merry way. However, the belief was already formed and can have a profound effect on her later life.

•

The majority of our BS are naturally updated and changed as we go through life. We learn how to walk, ride a bicycle, tie our shoes, read, drive a car, get a job, and so on. Most of our belief systems work for us in a positive way and help us navigate through life. However, when a belief is formed early and with strong emotions, it can remain unchanged in the subconscious until such time as it's consciously changed. It's these beliefs that are formed early in childhood and remain unchanged that cause us problems as adults.

Satan knows our weaknesses that are linked to our BS and he attacks our minds in those areas. He attacks us with his lies. Years ago, Dr. Bill Bright, the founder of Campus Crusade for Christ, International explained this battle for our minds this way. As Christians, we have both a spiritual nature and a carnal nature, and each has its own channel. Our spiritual nature listens to the Holy Spirit channel, while our carnal nature listens to the enemy channel. Many times a day we have to decide whom we will listen to: the Holy Spirit and truth, or the enemy and lies. We make the choice.

When the enemy begins to torment you with lies or tries to make you feel unworthy, turn the channel of your thoughts to the Holy Spirit channel and begin quoting Scripture to yourself and the enemy. That is what Jesus did when the enemy taunted Him and the enemy had to go away.

Remember what the Psalmist said, "Your Word have I hid in my heart, that I may not sin against You." (Psalm 119:11 NLV) Memorize and keep the Godly affirmations handy. When the voice of the enemy would have you believe lies, quickly turn your thoughts to God's truths.

That's what the next chapter is about: being able to discern the voices and knowing which one to listen to!

Your belief system is the actual set of precepts from which you live your daily life, those which govern your thoughts, words, and actions. Without these precepts you could not function, so in order to take this journey, and to give it some meaning, you must answer the following questions for yourself. It will help you find out where you are, and as with any journey it helps to know where you are starting. Please understand that this is not an easy thing for most people to do, but it is necessary to see ourselves as we truly are no matter how unpleasant this task may be. Even if you think you know the answers, please read the questions and think about the truthful answers that need to be given. If any part of what you believe is a lie, then you are not acting from a place of truth. For without acting in a way that is completely truthful, you will find that everything you do is a lie, therefore any attempt you might make toward resolving any problem would be in vain.

1) What do you believe?

2) Why do you believe it?

The answers to these questions (if we are truthful) define who we are, how we act, and what we truly believe, but we must be brutally honest. People are very strange when it comes to being honest with themselves. We have ways of deceiving ourselves into believing we did the right things, and of course, for the right reasons, but did we? As they say, nobility is not a birthright, it is defined by our actions, which are choices formed by our beliefs. Our beliefs are also choices. If you want to know what your true beliefs are, look at the things you do, the way you treat not just yourself and other people, but everything around you. Look at the way you interact or don't interact with others. Most importantly look at why, or the reasons behind why you do what you do.

In order to find out what belief system you have, or have adopted, certain questions must be asked since this is the most important aspect of defining who you are.

MAKE IT PERSONAL

1) As you review your life, what events strengthened some of your negative core beliefs about God? About yourself?

2) How have your belief systems impacted the way you see yourself?

3) Have you ever taken a good look at God's Word and what it says about you?

4) Have you given any thought at all to the belief system you have?

5) Did you make a conscious decision to believe what you

do or not?

6) Did you adopt your parents', spouse's, or others' belief systems because they were what you grew up with or just wanted to do?

7) If you did make a decision, did you make an informed decision, or did you just decide arbitrarily?

8) If you did make an informed decision, on what information did you base your decision?

9) What was the source of this information?

10) Was the source of the information just what you had heard from people who profess some sort of spiritual or religious practice? If so did you get your information from their pamphlets, info sheets, or instructional material?

11) Have you read the Bible for yourself?

12) If you haven't done these things, how important are you to yourself?

EXERCISE: How have your belief systems (negative and positive) shaped you?

_____

_____

_____

CHAPTER 4

WHEN DID WE BUY THE LIE?

E ach of us has bought into the lies of the enemy at one time or another. For most of us, it was when we were young. But before I get into how WE bought the lie, let me share how Eve, the first woman, bought the lie.

EVE BOUGHT THE LIE FIRST

"Jesus loves me this I know, for the Bible tells me so. Little ones to Him belong. They are weak but He is strong. Yes, Jesus loves me. Yes, Jesus loves me. Yes, Jesus loves me. The Bible tells me so."

This simple song and that catchy tune was something we sang in Sunday school as kids, or maybe it was just something that we have just heard at some point in our lives. Either way it is simple yet beautiful because it captures the Gospel in such a wonderful way.

Yet somewhere along the way for many of us, things changed. Like the snake did for Eve in the garden, doubt has been planted in our lives and has begun to corrupt for us the beautiful meaning of these simple words. You see the snake didn't convince Eve to eat the fruit, rather the snake planted doubt in Eve's mind that God was not looking out for her best interest. From there she bit the fruit in order to be self-sufficient from God, because in her mind God wasn't looking out for her any longer. She bought the lie that God really didn't love her the way He said He did. Many of you reading this are there, too.

Many of us have had doubt overshadow that simple truth in our lives that Jesus really does love us, and that He loves us unconditionally. Many of us have begun to think that God really isn't looking out for what's best for us. But take heart and hear this... *"For I am convinced that neither death nor life, neither angels nor demons, neither the present nor the future, nor any powers, neither height nor depth, nor anything else in all creation, will be able to separate us from the love of God that is in Christ Jesus our Lord."* (Romans 8:38-39)

Scripture indicates that the lie that changed the course of God's plan for us was sown by Satan, the father of lies (John 8:44). He was a murderer from the beginning. His weapon was the LIE perpetrated in Eden (Genesis 3:1-7). The lie was an attack upon the character of God and upon the genuineness and absolute authority of His holy Word. I think the best way to describe the premise and conclusion found in the lie at the garden is in my explanation below:

In a nutshell, the lie suggested by the enemy is that to make God's glory one's highest goal and obedience to Him one's life direction, would be to miss out on one's true potential for fulfillment, advancement, and freedom. The lie mistrusted God's character — it called into question His goodness and intentions toward mankind. As the lie suggested, if God's glory is not joined to man's highest good, humans have a rationale or justification for self-determination. The underlying thought process is that *you* may choose what you deem is best for yourself and *you* may choose right and wrong for yourself — for God is not absolutely trustworthy. The enemy continues with the lie that if you choose this path of self-direction, your world *will not* fall apart, *you will* succeed and you *will not* face death and damnation in hell.

The devil makes us believe that God's will expressed in His commandments is *not really* in the best interest of *our* happiness. God's threats are exaggerated — actually they are idle threats to keep us under His control. He's a micromanager. Who likes micro-managers!?

Now as a women's advocate for all roles in the kingdom, I want to clearly state that this book is not Eve bashing. This is what I believe from years of reading and re-reading the Bible, and I stand by it! The serpent didn't tempt Eve without tempting Adam. Adam was *with* Eve when Satan deceived her.

Genesis 3 says: "So when the woman saw that the tree

was good for food, and that it was a delight to the eyes, and that the tree was to be desired to make one wise, she took of its fruit and ate, and she also gave some to her husband *who was with her*, and he ate." (v. 6, emphasis added)

Earlier in the chapter, the story seems to suggest that the only two characters present are Eve and serpent, but verse 6 tells us that Eve's husband, Adam, was with her. Adam was the one who was commanded by God to not eat of the tree of knowledge of good and evil.

1Timothy 2:14 says: "Adam was not deceived, but the woman was deceived and became a transgressor." Both, of course, sinned, but the difference is that Adam willfully sinned, whereas Eve was captivated by Satan. She bought the lie and then sinned. Adam abdicated to his wife instead of standing up for her and rebuking the Devil; thus, he willfully disobeyed God.

We see this in God's punishment of Adam and Eve. He doesn't mention Eve disobeying him, but he does say to Adam: "Because you have listened to the voice of your wife and have eaten of the tree of which I commanded you, 'You shall not eat of it,' cursed is the ground because of you; in pain you shall eat of it all the days of your life..." (Gen. 3:17)

Adam is the one who bears the consequences, because he was the one commanded by God to not eat from the tree. He was responsible for protecting his wife, and he failed. In Genesis 2, before God creates Eve, he says to Adam: "You may surely eat of every tree of the garden, but of the tree of the knowledge of good and evil you shall not eat, for in the day that you eat of it you shall surely die." (v. 16-17)

When the serpent comes to Adam and Eve, he tempts them with a lie. Adam knows the truth, but Eve does not, *because she didn't hear God say it.* Satan introduces doubt and entangles Eve in deception and she unfortunately buys the lie, but Adam, either out of distrust for God, sheer disobedience, or even fear, chooses to do what he knows is wrong. I remember my old boss, the Rev. Ray Rivera mentioning how this is where our situation of captivity began and where that whole submission thing comes into play. Since Adam, the fallen nature of men dictates that we will abdicate more than we lead. God knew that women would naturally serve, but that men would naturally avoid responsibility. They have to be forced into it. I tend to agree with this

•

Actually, I really don't care to put blame on anyone. Do you know why? Because the facts are the facts. It is what it is and we just have to learn to deal with what is, instead of fighting about what was. I leave that up to the theologians in the academy. For me and I think for you too, we just want to know how we learn not to continue to make this mistake and buy the lies the enemy tells us. Learn from Eve so we can keep it moving in the right direction. Am I right?

One thing that the story of Eve and the garden shows us is that the Christian life is one of warfare. Many of us are so quick to point fingers but I can only imagine what any one of us would have done in the same situation. The truth is that there is the struggle with the flesh (Rom. 7:14-25) and there are temptations that arise throughout life. Given the fact that Christians endure one temptation after another, and, given the fact that history is littered with people and denominations that have succumbed to the lies of Satan, we really should try to understand Satan's methodology of deception... lies!

This is why the best place to examine his tactic and methodology is where Eve bought the lie in Genesis 3:1-6: "Now the serpent was more cunning than any beast of the field which the LORD God had made. And he said to the woman, 'Has God indeed said, 'You shall not eat of every tree of the garden?' And the woman said to the serpent, 'We may eat the fruit of the trees of the garden; but of the fruit of the tree which is in the midst of the garden, God has said, 'You shall not eat it, nor shall you touch it, lest you die.' Then the serpent said to the woman, 'You will not surely die. For God knows that in the day you eat of it your eyes will be opened, and you will be like God, knowing good and evil.' So when the woman saw that the tree was good for food, that it was pleasant to the eyes, and a tree desirable to make one wise, she took of its fruit and ate. She also gave to her husband with her, and he ate."

After telling Eve that God is a liar, that sin will not result in death, Satan next explains why God has lied and why Eve will not die. "For God knows that in the day that you eat of it your eyes will be opened, and you will be like God, knowing good and evil" (v. 5). Satan told Eve that God lied because he does not want her to have the wonderful blessing that attends the eating of the forbidden fruit. His statement to Eve clearly implies that an evil motive lies behind God's command. Satan told Eve that God is selfish; that He is not really concerned for her welfare. "Eve, the reason God told you not to eat the fruit is *not* because eating it will cause you to die. The real reason is that God is selfish. He doesn't want you to be like Him."

All of Satan's arguments lead straight to the bait: "the day you eat of it your eyes will be opened, and you will be like God knowing good and evil" (v. 5). Note once again Satan's carefully designed argument. Note the brilliant progression of deception. *First,* Satan asks an outwardly friendly question to show his concern, to gain Eve's trust all the while planting the seed of doubt in her heart. *Second,* Satan calls God a liar and then explicitly denies God's judgment for disobedience. *Third,* Satan attacks God's motive by implying that God is selfish and unconcerned for Eve's welfare. Then, *last* of all Satan sets before Eve the bait, the price, and the reward.

FOUR THINGS SATAN OFFERED EVE IN THE LIE

There are four things that should be noted regarding Satan's offer to Eve.

First, Satan offered Eve instant gratification: "The *day* you eat of it your eyes will be opened" (v. 5). God in the covenant of works had promised eternal life to Adam if he was obedient to God's word.

This covenant required sacrifice and obedience in the present in order to receive a reward in the future. If Adam and Eve were obedient, then at a God-ordained time God would have bestowed upon Adam and Eve eternal life. They would still be finite creatures but all possibility of a future fall into sin would have been forever removed by God. They could have partaken of the sealing ordinance by eating from the tree of life. God was in sovereign control of the bestowal of eternal life. Note the satanic philosophy regarding receiving a blessing. Satan taught that the blessing did not come from God. The reward existed independently of God's power and determination. Therefore, Satan rejected the biblical teaching regarding trust in God, obedience to His word, and patient submission to His providence. Satan taught that Eve should grasp the blessing immediately through her own power. The idea that the fruit could bless apart from God is a belief in magic. It is witchcraft and sorcery. "Look, Eve, you are in control of the blessing and not God. You can have your eyes opened and be like God this very day." The whole idea of obtaining instant gratification by disobeying God's law is the fundamental philosophy behind this present age. Paul wrote against this satanic thinking: God "'will render to each one according to his deeds:' eternal life to those who by patient continuance in doing good seek for glory, honor, and immortality; but to those who are self-seeking and do not obey the truth, but obey unrighteousness — indignation and wrath..." (Rom. 2:7-8).

Second, Satan told Eve that her eyes would be opened. "Eve, don't be so limited in your knowledge, understanding and perception. Here is an opportunity to expand your consciousness. Why should you be content with your puny, finite creaturely perception and knowledge when you can have so much more just by eating the fruit?"

Third, Satan then told Eve why her eyes would be opened: "You will be like God." Satan told Eve that the path to dominion and blessing is not through obedience to God and His law-word, but through going beyond her created-beingness and finiteness. According to Satan man is not to concern himself with obedience, submission, or ethics. Isaiah 14:14 says that Satan fell because he wanted to be like the most High. He set before Eve the same blasphemous notion. "Eve, if you eat the fruit you will be like God. You will be all-knowing. You will have equality with God. You will no longer be dependent upon Him for meaning, ethics, and truth. You will be self-sufficient. If you eat the fruit you will be sovereign. Then you and not God can call the shots."

Satan did not want man to obey God but to become god — determining for himself reality, meaning, and ethics. This satanic philosophy lies behind all rebellion in this world.

Fourth, Satan told Eve that if she becomes like God, then she will know good and evil. Adam and Eve will be like God because they will define or determine for themselves what is good and what is evil. This interpretation is confirmed by Genesis 3:22 NIV: "And the Lord God said, "The man has now become like one of us, knowing good and evil."

Eve, following Satan's lead, assumed that she lived in an impersonal environment. She accepted Satan's premise that God's word could not be trusted and that therefore the only reliable method for achieving truth and knowledge was human autonomy. Eve would have to seek independence from her creator.

Once she accepted all these satanic assumptions, eating

the fruit to be like God in order to determine for herself good and evil was but a small step, for she had already eaten the fruit in her heart. Note, sin always begins in the heart or mind.

WHAT WE CAN LEARN FROM THIS STORY

Although Satan's temptation of Eve was very cunning and deceptive he did not force Eve to eat the forbidden fruit. She had to buy the lie, thus Eve cooperated with the devil and allowed him to lead her into sin. All believers should carefully note and understand what Eve did that led her into disobedience. There are a number of things that Eve did that all Christians should avoid.

1. *Eve engaged herself in a dialogue with the enemy (Satan) on his terms.* Satan directed the subject matter and controlled the conversation. Eve allowed herself to be taken into ungodly territory. Eve is approached by a snake that talks and questions God's word. Since Eve was under the authority of Adam she should have immediately consulted her husband when confronted by such unsavory circumstances. Whenever Christians are confronted by a situation that is even questionable the best thing to do is step back and seek the counsel of the Scriptures and other believers. I have a personal advisory board that I seek out for counsel, and they have helped me tremendously throughout the years.

2. *Eve set herself up as the ultimate authority in the interpretation of reality.* When Satan told Eve that God had lied, that she would not die, he clearly was contradicting what God had said. The moment that Satan called God a liar, Eve should have rebuked him with a "get thee behind me Satan." But, instead she committed herself to a position of independence, a position of self-sufficiency from God and His word. She decided to examine what God had said and

what Satan had said and then make a decision. Eve took God's word and Satan's word and placed them on the same level. She believed that she should be the ultimate authority and judge between them.

Note, that in autonomously determining whether or not it was ethical to eat the forbidden fruit, Eve acted as both a realist and a rationalist. Gosh, something I have struggled with on many occasions myself in my own faith journey! I'm so real sometimes I can talk myself out of God's blessings! We women think we are so smart sometimes! So how did Eve act as a realist, you ask? Instead of trusting in God's authoritative word she decided to study the tree. She looked at the tree. She noted that it was good for food and pleasant to the eyes. Yeah, I know you can see yourself doing the same thing! Don't lie! I ain't buying it!

Eve interpreted the information she gathered with her senses. She decided based on this information that the tree was desirable to make one wise. She had already rejected God's word and had assumed that she existed in an impersonal environment. Eve believed that the only method for obtaining truth was to go on a fact gathering mission. Aren't we women like that? I do that all the time and now with Google, we are dangerous! But we have to know that when it comes to the Word of God, "He said it, we have to believe it, and that settles it!"

Now Eve was also a rationalist because she believed that reason could discover truth and accurately determine reality apart from God's word. Adam and Eve were created in the image of God (Gen. 1:27) and thus were different from the brute beasts. They were given the ability to use reason and logic. Man's ability to reason is essential in his task of dominion over the earth (Gen. 1:26). Logic is essential for communication, math, philosophy, theology, science, and so on. However, human reason was never meant to be used independent from God's special revelation. Man was given reasoning capabilities in order: to commune with God, to understand God's word, to carry out God's commandments, and to obediently create a God-loving civilization throughout the earth. Using human reason apart from God's word and to judge it is a denial of our total dependence upon God and His revelation for truth, knowledge, meaning, and ethics. Before the fall, God had direct communication with Adam and Eve in the garden. God's commandment to Adam was to be obeyed solely on the basis of God's authority.

For a man to place God in the dock and stand as judge over His word is proof that man has already abandoned God and His word for autonomy, for self-law. Proverbs 1:7 (NLV) says: "The fear of the Lord is the beginning of much learning. Fools hate wisdom and teaching."

The Word goes on to tell us in Proverbs 3:5 that we should trust God and not rely on our understanding. Reason used apart from God is constantly used to rationalize sin. Sin, however, is never rational. I know I can get a few amens for that! How many of us rationalized our way to do what our flesh wanted just to make us feel better? So you see, we aren't so different from Mother Eve after all. That is why we have to learn!

3. Eve coveted that which was unlawful. She lusted after the forbidden fruit. She stared at the fruit and contemplated how she would benefit from eating it. A great deal of sin begins with the lust of the eyes: adultery, fornication, theft, kidnapping, and so on. There is the example of Achan: "When I saw among the spoils a beautiful Babylonian garment, two hundred shekels of silver, and a wedge of gold weighing fifty shekels, I coveted them and took them" (Josh 7:21).

David also was guilty of lusting with his eyes: "Then it happened one evening that David arose from his bed and walked on the roof of the king's house. And from the roof he saw a woman bathing, and the woman was very beautiful to behold. So David sent and inquired about the woman" (2

Sam 11:2). The apostle John warned believers not to love the world by saying: "For all that is in the world — the lust of the flesh, the lust of the eyes, and the pride of life — is not of the Father but is of the world" (1 Jn. 2:16). What Eve, Achan, and David were all guilty of was staring at what they knew was sinful and off-limits and contemplating the pleasures of sin in the mind. Staring at the forbidden fruit and toying with sin in the mind is spiritual suicide. When you are on a diet, you do not go into a donut shop and stare at the donuts and fantasize about them.

4. *Eve was guilty of sinful pride.* Eve's decision to determine for herself what was right and what was wrong was rooted in pride. It was the height of pride and arrogance to think that she — a finite creature — could be like the Almighty. "Pride goes before the destruction and a haughty spirit before a fall" (Pr. 16:18). Eve was full of pride when she decided that she deserved the fruit and the supposed blessings that it contained. The same type of pride lies behind all flagrant sin.

Eve's decision to forsake God's word and do her own thing involved unbelief. Eve knew God's word. She clearly had an understanding of God's ban. Her problem was not a lack of understanding but a lack of trust. *As it is with us.* Eve did not believe God's word. She did not have faith in God. *As it is with us.* If Eve had really believed God's word, she would not have placed it on the same level as Satan's word. She would not have subjected it to her self-sufficient reasoning. Eve would have obeyed it without question. The Bible emphasizes the relationship between faith and obedience. "He who says, 'I know Him,' and does not keep His commandments, is a liar, and the truth is not in him" (1 John. 2:4). Satan's careful planning and cunning deception coupled with Eve's willingness to listen and then cooperate with this deception was a disaster for mankind, for: "Eve took of its fruit and ate. She also gave to her husband with her and he ate" (Gen.

3:6). Satan did not take the fruit and put it in Eve's mouth. He can tempt but he cannot force. Adam and Eve were totally responsible for their actions. "But each one is tempted when he is drawn away by his own desires and enticed. Then, when desire has conceived, it gives birth to sin; and sin, when it is full-grown, brings forth death" (Jas. 1:14-15).

WHERE I BOUGHT THE LIE

So we all know Eve bought the lie in the Garden. But what you don't know is where *I* bought the lie. When I started working on this book and really when I crashed into Calvary and started looking at myself, I realized I bought the lie when I was in church in my pre-teen years more so than when I was a child. I've shared the traumatic story of the hickey. My pastor said I was a prostitute and my church family ostracized me. All of that formed very strong belief systems.

Now while I had already formed BS as a child that would make it easy for me to buy the lies during my pre-teen years, I really didn't realize the blows of my early years as much as the cognitive awareness I had when I was a pre-teen. What follows are the major life blows that helped me to see how full of it I was. *It* being ungodly BS. While there have been many things that have happened to me and shaped me, the following life blows are the ones that were the heavy hitters from my perspective.

•

I was born to a Puerto Rican woman who came from her isla at the age of 18, met and married my father, who was a barber and their union created the lovely me. What my mom and I didn't know was that by the age of 2, he would leave me and mom broke, busted, and disgusted with life. For the most part, I didn't remember him, so that helped with the missing "daddy" part. From 2-10 years old, I don't recall anything other than visiting family for the holidays and doing the typical Latino things like cooking with family, playing bomba y plena for parties, waking up to La Mega Se Pega music, and smelling King Pine on Saturday mornings while my mom cleaned the house. I fell in love with coffee at an early age due to the mesmerizing smell of Bustelo. Don't know if I attribute that to selective amnesia or if there really wasn't anything that extraordinary to remember... good or bad. When I hit my teen years all that changed.

•

Before I tell you what lies I bought, I have to tell you about the BS I formed. Stay with me.

Remember the hickey story? My church put me on punishment for six months. I could not participate in church activities and members were supposed to stay away from me. After the six months were up, I went back to church since I was still in contact with some people. Many of them were my community. In that time, many Christians learned that we were not to socialize with non-Christians in an effort to avoid getting contaminated, so they were my only friends. I still in some way believed in the promise of what the church could be even though I didn't see any evidence of it so far in the people I expected it from the most. Namely, the pastor, the deacons, etc.

From that time until I went to college, I had a deep-seated distrust of church people. They were not safe people. They didn't give people a chance. I learned to hide my true self, and act the way they wanted me to act, the way *they* acted... perfect.

I eventually went on to college but I never forgot the hurt I experienced. I think a part of me was cynical about church. Interestingly enough I didn't blame God for all that. When I went to college, I acted out on some of the things people *prophe-lied* over me. I figured if they think I did it, I might as well do it! *I figured I would explore the other side of things, the "sinful" side.* And so I did.

When I went to college, I made sure it was away from NYC. I went first to SUNY-Binghamton and then transferred over to SUNY-New Paltz. All for a guy, truth be told. When I was there I partied a lot, joined a sorority and became pretty popular on campus. I thought that was the key. It really wasn't. To make things cheaper, I actually lived with my boyfriend for most of my college years until my last year when my sorority sisters and I created the Delta house and shared the expenses renting a home in the area. It was during my last year in college, that my boyfriend at that time (who was also a church boy run amok), and I broke up.

But you know what, God knows everything. Today he is happily married with three kids, married for as long as I have been, and it's all good. I'm even Facebook friends with his wife! God gave us both what we needed just not with *each other*!

Eventually, I dated and married one of the young men I grew up with in church. (I was a church girl, after all, so all my serious boyfriends were church boys.) Although his mom was a pillar in the church and deacon around the time all that happened to me in my teen years, she saw me, *the real me* in spite of my past mistakes and thankfully his mother was a *real* Godly woman who didn't let that little teenage mishap jade her about me. She just told me when we announced to the family we were getting serious that she would pray, and if I were meant for her son, it would happen. Isn't that what anyone would ask for? After all, if she prayed and he wasn't for me, she saved me a headache, too!

•

We married on May 18, 1990 and three months later started working with the youth ministry in my church on the Lower East Side. Yes, the same church where I had suffered such hurt at the hands of my leaders. After seven years of marriage, we gave birth to my first son, Samuel Eliu Rios on June 7, 1997. A great pregnancy almost turned into a dramatic birth when I had to be wheeled into the ER because he was going into distress as the umbilical cord was wrapped around his neck. Something I was told happens a lot in pregnancies but easily detected. After a C-section delivery, my son never really gave me much more drama. Now 15 years old, he has been healthy most of his life and after being homeschooled for all his middle school years, just entered a private Christian high school and is the lead keyboard player at his school and is on the worship team at my church. I praise God for that!

On September 22, 1999, my second son, Daniel Jeremiah "DJ" Rios, was born at a New York hospital. After an incredibly spiritually fulfilling women's retreat which I coordinated every year through my organization, the Center for Emerging Female Leadership, I gave birth three months early (at 26 weeks). After the initial reaction of being told that I was 8 centimeters dilated and that their priority was my life (meaning not his) and that he only had a fifty-fifty chance of survival, I reverted to the feeling of being God's stepchild, otherwise why after such a powerful event where women were ministered to, where the guest speaker specifically prayed for my unborn child, would this happen to me? I had stayed in town an extra few days after returning from the retreat to help plan the pastoral installation into full-time ministry for another of his women warriors going into full-time ministry, my sister-in-love, Enid Rios Rivera.

It gave me great joy to plan such a significant event for such a significant woman in my life, who was one of the few who believed in me since I was a child, who saw promise and potential in me, even after "the mark." I was thrilled to be there but had no idea that this would also be the awful beginning to my second son's life and one of the most traumatic experiences in mine. I also didn't know that it was going to get a whole lot worse. Real fast.

My husband had to be called by his sister while he was still in Florida (where we had moved in January of 1998 with my firstborn). When he was told I had had the baby and everything was fine, he didn't believe it. He knew it was too early. He thought his sister was not sharing the truth that the baby had died. She didn't give him all the information so as not to make him a nervous wreck as he flew back up North with my other son in tow. Later that night he arrived at the hospital. I was thankful to have him by my side, but sad I could not deliver a full-term baby. That's baby number two he did not get to see come out of me. His dream denied. Another dream shattered for me, this time, a dream to give my husband *two* healthy children.

The doctors had checked me, my placenta, and the baby. Nothing could be found that could point to a reason why I gave birth so early. They said 80 percent of pregnancies are early deliveries. That didn't make me feel better. Why me? My baby was 2 pounds at birth. When I got to see him the next day, he was translucent and looked like a baby chicken. I cried as I watched him in his incubator. There is something about a mother's love that would do anything to make all the pain stop for her children. For the first time since I was that 15-year-old on discipline, I felt helpless.

•

As a recovering Type A, ENTJ personality I did not like feeling helpless. Devoid of a solution. My husband and I prided ourselves on being solution-oriented people and yet in this very real family situation, we had nada, zilch, zero. And it seemed God had forgotten me *yet again.* That old BS kicked up potently.

I tried to fight those thoughts. I talked to myself. I encouraged myself as David did in the Psalms. Even though I knew underneath the layers of my soul, I had this ingrained BS that God goes on vacation when you need Him the most, I so very much wanted to believe otherwise. So I searched the scriptures. I put on healing scripture music for DJ. I prayed. I even prayed kneeling because the hermanas made it seem like that was the holiest way to do it. I fasted. I did everything ritually biblical I knew how to do.

But my BS remained.

•

Seven months after his birth, he was allowed to leave the hospital but he was leaving with a diagnosis of hydrocephalus (too much water on the brain) caused by a staph infection that the medical personnel treated too late, approximately 10 hours too late since by the time they went to give him antibiotics, the infection had already gone into his cerebral spinal fluid and spread to his brain. He eventually would be diagnosed with cerebral palsy, cortical blindness, scoliosis, bone atrophy, and failure to thrive, just to name a few.

I saw all that had happened with my son's birth and his diagnosis as further evidence of my BS that God had abandoned me. I let Him know exactly how I felt.

The day I left the hospital I remember telling God, *"You are the one that looks like a fool because I said **you** would heal him."* I remember taking down the hand-made posters from his crib that had scriptures on them proclaiming healing. I also remember walking down the corridors of the hospital with DJ in his car seat, feeling like I had my tail between my legs. *"Yeah, I'm certain, I'm God's stepchild,"* I thought to myself. Another negative BS strengthened.

For the next two years I lived in and out of the hospital. Thankfully I worked for the best boss I've ever had, the Rev. Dr. Raymond Rivera at the Latino Pastoral Action Center, who was a compassionate man and allowed me to work *from the hospital* while planning conferences, writing grants, and whatever else I needed to do so I could get paid (since I needed the money)! My assistant, Cielo Delgado, God bless her, would come to the hospital and bring me my messages and work. There were even times she stayed in the hospital with me to keep me company. But it was a rough time for my family. My husband was alone most of the time taking care of my oldest while I was in the hospital with my youngest. It was during this time that DJ's neurosurgeon hinted that what happened to him (and numerous other things that happened that I won't get into) were negligence. It was then that I knew I had to pursue legal action. Eight years later we won the case and got justice for DJ! But I would have given anything to just have a normal baby.

On a Wednesday — August 1, 2001 — my youngest had a febrile seizure while home. We lived in the Bronx at the time and he was coughing up blood. It was late at night and he was sleeping with me so I could watch him closely, while my husband slept in the living room. No matter what we did DJ could not be comforted and the fever would not go down so we called an ambulance. He ended up having to go back to the neurosurgeon because he had a shunt infection. Had we not taken him in they said his brain would have fried and he would have died. So there I was in the hospital AGAIN. My life was about to get beyond belief ugly in a matter of days. That Saturday, August 4, after details I will spare you, I found out something that threw my marriage into a tailspin, so much so that it was bound for divorce!

Now, let's be real. I wanted to kill my husband. I didn't because I wanted to stay out of prison. No, I'm not going to lie and say it was because God's love was all over me. I did have dreams of hiring a hit team. While I was in the hospital caring for my son who almost died, I found out this very painful news. Wow! I didn't think anything could feel any worse other than getting knifed or shot at point blank range. I specifically remember looking up at the ceiling in the hospital room and screeching, with my voice telling God, *"Why don't you just kill me!"*

I couldn't do more than that because as a semi-private room, there was another person in there. But I just wanted to die. Seriously, I literally contemplated suicide. The enormity of the pain was unbearable. There weren't enough tears I could cry, the fetal position did me no justice, and even alcohol couldn't make me forget.

In the middle of dealing with a sick child, I now had to begin preparations for divorce. After doing all the talking with the transgressors and our pastors at the time (who also happened to be family and YES this did affect that relationship too for a while), I had decided a divorce was the way to go. I gave my husband until September 30 to find a new place to live. I had resolved in my mind that there was no turning back. I mean, I was dealing with OUR child and he was out dealing with his pain in not such a noble way. I couldn't wrap my head around that, no matter who he begged to talk to me to convince me to change my mind. I considered it a miracle that I hadn't killed him and that was the only miracle he was going to get.

My BS was in full effect. My mother had told me so many times that all men are pigs. And I had seen what I felt to be God's absence at my most critical times. My BS opened the way for the enemy to feed me the lies that I couldn't rely on my God because of my man.

•

Then September 11 happened. It paused a nation. A nation was gripped with its own pain and I also was dealing with my own personal hell. Yet, it made me stop to think that maybe it could have been me on the other side. I stopped to ask, "Do I love this man? Can I forgive him *in time?*" During this time period, not surprisingly, we had church people talk about us. I was made to feel uncomfortable in my own church (yes the same church that made me feel uncomfortable when I was a teen), and people walked away from us as if we had leprosy. Since the other culprit in the picture *never* showed remorse, *never* asked for forgiveness and *never* left the church to allow us to heal (especially since it was our church first!), we decided to leave to find another place to heal. Needless to say, we are still together. I'm thankful because we celebrated 22 years of marriage and 24 years together (1 year dating, 1 year engaged) in 2012! And I can truly say our marriage is stronger than ever. Disclaimer: *Not the best way to go about getting a strong marriage so don't try this at home!*

There you have it in the most concise way I can deliver it, the major blows of my life. All these situations reinforced the belief systems in me that:

1) God must not hear my prayers.

2) Church people don't really care.

3) Church people won't be there for you when you really need them.

4) Church people can't and should never be trusted.

5) Church people do what they tell you not to do. They just learn not to get caught.

6) I'm God's stepchild.

7) God must go on vacation when you really need Him.

It was after all these life blows that I started to do some serious never done before soul-searching. I read a lot, prayed a lot, and talked with a select group of friends regularly who were also venturing on the edge of their belief systems. My faith had taken a serious hit, and I knew I had to find a way to get it back.

This soul-searching changed my life. I learned from reading the biographies of some great soldiers of the faith and their great pains to believe God and what He says I am and what I can do.

I knew then that if I was going to make it in this life with my mind intact, I had to find out what I really, truly believed about God and form a theology for myself. I had to build myself up again with his Word (Ps. 119:28) and then start acting like I'm a believer with my mind, actions, and forward movement dictated by the Word. "Therefore everyone who hears these words of mine and puts them into practice is like a wise man who built his house on the rock." (Matt. 7:24, NIV)

WHERE DID YOU BUY THE LIE?

So where did you buy the lie? I've always shared and I'm sure you have heard this before that everybody has a story. It is while God is writing the chapters of our lives that we get caught up in the snare of the enemy. Paul wrote that we must be watchful that we don't fall into the "snare" of the devil. "Moreover he must have a good report of them which are without; lest he fall into reproach and the snare of the devil" (I Timothy 3:7). What is the snare of the devil? It is his deception, his lie. Each time Jesus was tempted, he answered the temptation with, "It is written" (Matthew 4:6, 7, 10). Each time we buy one of the devil's lies, it roots a belief system, an ungodly belief system in us that will then function as our decision-making core.

Paul also wrote that we are to stand against the "wiles" of the devil. "Put on the full armor of God, so that you can take your stand against the devil's schemes." (Ephesians 6:11 NIV). What are the "schemes" of the devil? These are lies! We must stand in the truth of who God is and who we are in Christ. You probably bought a lie when God didn't perform the way you expected him to, like I did. That's when we usually do.

We are also to be careful for the "devices" of the devil. "That no advantage may be gained over us by Satan: for we are not ignorant of his devices." (II Corinthians 2:11 ASV). What are the "devices" of the devil? The context of the passage suggests that the problem is unforgiveness.

However, unforgiveness is based upon **a lie** that we must get even to be at peace. Did you buy that one? Can you retrace that point in time? I remember when I forgave my husband (which came sooner than when I forgave all the other folks involved). I had to understand that unforgiveness was a prison that was going to keep ME trapped. I had to realize that my destiny was too important to let people who probably had moved on and sleeping soundly have free rent in my brain. I don't think anyone gets to go through this world without having a situation they have to forgive someone for. Don't buy the lie of the enemy. Forgive. It's for you, not for them.

•

Maybe you bought the lie when someone accused you of something that wasn't true, or labeled you something that you weren't. For me, it was when a PASTOR said I had a mark of a prostitute, labeling me not only in my mom's eyes but even in my own. Yet the Word says, we are to extinguish all the flaming arrows of the enemy. "In addition to all this, take up the shield of faith, with which you can extinguish all the flaming arrows of the evil one" (Ephesians 6:16 NIV). What are the "flaming arrows" of the devil? Those false accusations about us, or even God, and His Word. They are **lies**! When you hold on to faith, based upon the truth of the Word, it puts out all the flaming arrows of the devil.

MAKE IT PERSONAL

1) What are the **lies** the enemy is using to attack you?

2) What **truths** from Scripture can you use to combat the **lies**?

EXERCISE: Add to the list of negative belief systems you wrote about in the first two exercises. Let's go deeper. This time, don't stop at three. Write down *every* ungodly belief system you have. Then write down at least one memory that created or reinforced this belief system. Use additional paper, if necessary. When you are done, look at the sheet. That's the

BS you are full of and need to combat today!

_____

_____

_____

CHAPTER 5

KNOWING WHOM TO LISTEN TO

B y now you have already guessed what I am trying to tell you. We limit our ability to reach our potential, live a joyful life, and impact our destiny when we listen to the lies of the enemy. The reason so many of us buy his lies is because we have ungodly BS stored in our minds based on a lie Satan told us and we believed. One thing will never change throughout our Christian journey: We will always have a choice to listen to Satan or to God.

One thing I have heard over and over again when I have ministered in my church or through Center for Emerging Female Leadership events is this: "How do we know what voice to listen to?" "How do we distinguish between voices?" I am going to go into three voices we have to decipher in our journey. God's, the devil's, and our own.

Each has its own characteristics, which help us distinguish between them. The reason knowing who you are listening to is so important is because there is a progression from deception to bondage in our belief systems and it doesn't happen overnight. We pride ourselves on not falling for an outright lie, but Satan doesn't work like that, anyway.

He just wants to get us involved in a conversation. A conversation where we listen to a few twisted statements or entertain just a little bit of doubt. Remember, this is how Eve got deceived in the garden. She *listened* to the lies that Satan told her.

•

It never really seems harmless to just listen, especially for those of us who like answers, so we research and do the logical things. Listening to hear him out, to see what he has to say, seems like the logical thing to do sometimes. Listening in and of itself is not disobedience BUT listening to something that we know is contrary to the Word of God puts us in a place that is dangerous, a slippery slope that leads to defiance of the things of God and yes, ultimately to our spiritual and in some cases, even physical death.

We are surrounded by lies all the time. It is our duty as believers to guard our minds and reject those things that promote ungodly beliefs because they will shape us more than we think. The way the voices come to us is through television, magazines, movies, music, friends, bus ads, you name it! And remember this: There are no harmless lies. A lie is a lie is a lie. You can't listen and entertain a lie and come out intact. The seed has been deposited. Eve's first mistake was not eating the fruit; her first mistake was listening to the father of lies. When we hear the voice of Satan he will want us to live with the lie, believe the lie, and then act on the lie. That is what Eve did and that is what we have been doing but you and I are making a resolution to not buy the lie anymore right? That means we need to discern the voices.

YOUR VOICE

Your voice will sound like your voice (if you have an accent, it will have one too). It will have the same inflections and will whimper about your own previous fleshly desires. Tell it to shut up. It ain't easy to die to self, but you can do it. If you want two opposing things at once, that's another sign that you know it's not God. Double-mindedness (James 1:8) is the red flag that you are not on a stable path. The Spirit is the only voice that is dependable and that will guide you into truth (John 16:13).

THE DEVIL'S VOICE

When the devil or another evil spirit is speaking to you one or more of the following will be notable:
• *Confusion.* For where envying and strife is, there is confusion and every evil work (James 3:16). God is not the

author of confusion. (1 Corinthians 14:33)

• *Condemnation.* There is therefore now no condemnation to them which are in Christ Jesus. (Romans 8:1)

• *Fear.* For God has not given us a spirit of fear, but of power and of love and of a sound mind. (2 Timothy 1:7)

When the devil speaks, he comes at you with the *opposite of truth* or what God said. He is the father of *lies* remember (John 8:44). He is also the *tempter* (Matthew 4:3); God doesn't tempt any man (James 1:13). He will also not say that Jesus came in the flesh (1 John 4:1-6). He may try to *deceive* you by adding to what God said (Genesis 3:1-5) like he did with Eve in the garden.

One of the devil's major tricks is *doubt.* He even tried to pull that one over on Jesus. "IF you are the Son of God..." (Matthew 4:3,6). Do what Jesus did: Use scripture to kick him out! I remember using that when I had my premature son. IF you are God you will heal DJ before he leaves this hospital. IF, is a major doubt indicator.

Satan, Lucifer, Beelzebub, the Evil One... we all know him by various names if we were good little Sunday school girls and have all sorts of ideas, myths, and notions about the Prince of Darkness. Some people think he is only a concept and not really a living entity, while others see him as an unrelenting supernatural creature with untold powers to curse, possess, dominate, and control.

Well some of these ideas are true while others are erroneous. Some of us like to blame the devil for all the bad things that happen to us. I've heard it numerous times in the Latino church where I grew up, hermanas saying "aye ese Diablo malo!" (Man, that bad devil!). It's been used for everything from a bad hair day to a flat tire. Yet we also are blinded by the fact that we are ultimately the ones responsible for everything that goes on with us and our world. You see, much of what the devil does himself... is nothing. Let me put it another way... the devil talks. He talks and talks and talks.

And who listens? We do.

We are the ones who listen and *believe* him. WE are the ones who buy his lies!

He whispers of the dangers of what may happen to us, so we become afraid. He points out the faults of others, so we spread gossip, prejudice, and stereotyping. He talks to us about how we are being taken advantage of, so we become angry.

Of course, a bit of healthy fear, questioning, and skepticism is natural so that we can learn and maneuver through our lives, but the devil wants us obsessed, irrational, and preoccupied.

Yes the devil does cause chaos, but through us. He himself doesn't have to lift a finger. We do all the work. Much the troubles of the world are because of us. But the devil tries to get us to blame God for our troubles.

"Why does God allow starvation in the world?" The question is... why are we allowing these people to starve? *"But all the wars and poverty?"* Guess who started the wars and allows poverty? Us. *"God is punishing me! The landlord is kicking me out."* Well... if you paid your bills...

Our selfishness, our greed, our corruption, our unwillingness to do the right thing or work with each other is why we have problems. Satan tells us to blame God, but we are responsible because we listen to the devil more than we listen to God and judging from the news, Satan truly does have a powerful grip on the world.

Yet, the devil is stuck on a stool in the corner... only barking at us.

Oh, it's easy to recognize the voice of Satan. He uses the same tactics all the time. He's not into change and why should he be? We've been buying his lies since the garden. He's pretty good at it and we're pretty predictable. His voice is always critical, negative, making excuses, divisive, distrustful, frustrated, frantic, impatient, selfish, fault-finding... his voice always tries to bring out the worst in us.

"Look at that selfish witch... you should get back at her." "Everyone else is doing it, what's wrong with it?" "No one loves you, you're alone in the world." "Don't get involved, it's none of your business." "Look at those people, they are sneaky, they stick together, and take advantage of us... we've got to stop them!"

You see the devil just talks, but we believe him... and do his work. He gets our minds going. He tells us to be afraid, he tells us to be discontent, he tells us to distrust others, he tells us to care only for ourselves... he just goes on and on and on and on. And we repeat his words to ourselves and others.

Being a Christian doesn't make us immune to the voice of the devil and even the most faithful servants of God fall for the devil's words. We have allowed his voice to govern our thoughts. We have allowed his voice to drown out God's voice.

God's voice is sweet. God's voice is hopeful. God's voice seeks to change things for the better, to make things stronger and more beautiful. Following the voice of God helps us discard the ugly parts of ourselves. The devil seeks to make those ugly parts greater. He wants us angrier, pettier, more selfish, more stagnant, more confused... he wants it ALL: Everything that is counter to the Fruits of the Spirit and the Love Commandments of God:

"But the fruit of the Spirit is love, joy, peace, patience, kindness, goodness, faithfulness, gentleness and self-control. Against such things there is no law" - Galatians 5:22-23

"'Love the Lord your God with all your heart and with all your soul and with all your mind.' This is the first and greatest commandment. And the second is like it: 'Love your neighbor as yourself.' All the Law and the Prophets hang on these two commandments." — Matthew 22: 37-40

The devil has even talked us into believing that all the

good things from God... are really BAD things.

"*Love, joy, peace? What, are you naive? Those unattainable, unrealistic fairy tale ideals are foolishness...that goes along with teddy bears, happy faces, sunflowers, and angels... simplistic, juvenile...stupid. LOVE only causes PAIN and DISAPPOINTMENT. If you believe in those things then you will be trampled over like roadkill...it's a dog-eat-dog world. Get your head out of the sand. Nice guys finish last. Every man for himself.*"

Unfortunately many of us rarely hear the voice of God, because God's voice is a whisper. It is drowned out by all these other loud mouths! But if we listen, we can hear it.

GOD'S VOICE

God's voice has love, patience, understanding, and compassion. It is counter to the ways of the world. God's voice asks for your action. He asks you to get up and serve Him and go against the words, the lies of Satan. God's voice asks us to do anything that will bring His love to the world, no matter how small. God's voice is very quiet just behind the devil's in-your-face shouting. You can barely hear Him, but He is saying to you... "*Listen to Me. Trust Me. Be patient. Be kind. Let your pain and sorrows go. Lift someone up. Accept someone no one else accepts. I love you, so love others, too!*"

That is God's voice desiring us to be healed, wanting us to get out of ourselves and to reach out in love to spread His hope. And the more we listen to the voice of God, the more His voice will grow stronger and the voice of the devil will become a faint background chatter.

Here are some things the Bible says about you that need to become things *you say about yourself.* Start every day by confessing these core truths to replace the ungodly BS you currently carry — and soon they will become the Godly belief systems that guide your life and decisions!

• I am crucified with Christ and I no longer live, but Christ lives in me. (Galatians 2:20)
• The Son has set me free. I am free indeed! (John 8:36)
• My body is the temple of the Holy Spirit. (1 Corinthians 6:19)
• I can do all things through Christ who gives me strength. (Philippians 4:13)
• He who began a good work in me will be faithful to complete it. (Philippians 1:6)
• There is now no condemnation for those who are in Christ Jesus. (Romans 8:1)
• Nothing can ever separate me from the love of God in Christ Jesus. (Romans 8:38-39)
• In all things God works for the good of those who love him. (Romans 8:28)
• God is faithful. He will not let me be tempted beyond what I can bear. (1 Corinthians 10:13)
• God has not given me a spirit of fear, but of power, love, and a sound mind. (2 Timothy 1:7)
• My light and momentary troubles are achieving for me an eternal glory that far outweighs them all. (2 Corinthians 4:17)
• He is able to do immeasurably more than all I ask or imagine, according to his power that is at work within me. (Ephesians 3:20)
• God is for me! Who can be against me? (Romans 8:31)

When you say what God says, you begin to think what God thinks and you become full of His Word which then in turn becomes your new core belief system. So let this be your confession of faith. And let it be the foundation on which you build your new life, a new life built upon Godly core beliefs.

This is not about the power of positive thinking. It's not

your good thoughts that will turn your life around. It's not about the power of attraction. It's God's power that will turn your life around. He's just asking you to believe He is who he says He is, believe you are who He says you are, and then live like you believe those things.

Does that mean bad things will stop happening? No. But it does mean you will experience many more victories than losses because the Word of God is at work in you and you are seeing yourself the way He sees you. That makes all the difference in the world!

How much power Satan has, is up to you. You have the ability to tune him out.

RECAP

Your Voice — fleshly desires, double-mindedness, and/or hesitation

Devil's Voice — confusion, condemnation, fear, lies, temptations, deceits, and/or doubt

God's Voice — radically joyful, optimistic and against all conventions of the world, it speaks of love, peace, forgiveness, reconciliation, and healing

Make an action plan based on the way each voice speaks. Your action plan should look like this:

THOUGHT	SPEAKING VOICE	MY ACTION
"I deserve to hurt those who hurt me"	Satan	*Read the word* Rom 12:19 "Do not take revenge, my friends, but leave room for God's wrath, for it is written: 'It is mine to avenge; I will repay,' says the Lord." *Pump up my playlist with music*

MAKE IT PERSONAL

1) *Do you ever take the time to analyze the voices you hear?*

2) What are the voices that you hear telling you?

3) Are you able now to discern amongst the voices? How do you know God's voice?

EXERCISE: Think about the voices you have listened to in the past week. Analyze them based on what you've just learned. Whose voices have you been listening to this week?

_____

_____

_____

CHAPTER 6

A LOOK AT THE LIES WE BUY

There are so many lies that we buy from the enemy of our soul. I'm tired of seeing people held back from the life God wants for them because their belief systems (BS) have been rooted in lies like some that you will you read about here. Listen, I can write about this because like you, I had also bought into the lie. This is my story just as much as it is yours. It is my struggle, just like it is yours. But education is so important in this battle with Satan. Of course, this is not an all-exhaustive list of the lies he comes up with but one thing is for sure, he does use the same thing over and over again based on the BS already rooted in our minds and hearts. I'll be sharing some of the lies I bought into but I know there are many, many more.

Lies About God

GOD IS NOT A GOOD GOD

These are the lies Satan loves to start with. This is the lie that ultimately messed up Eve and honestly the lie that messed me up for a while. The reason we fall for this lie is because life is full of challenges. An illness, a death of a loved one, a financial setback or a problem with a child can make us wonder if God really has our best interests at heart. This is one of the most persuasive lies that Satan has ever devised: *the lie that God is not good.* I know about that one personally because I believed this lie for a while. Especially after DJ's birth and the tryst my husband had with another woman. I definitely did not think God was good during that time in my life.

Nothing is more crucial than what you and I believe about God. In fact, what we believe about God is foundational to everything else about our lives. So if my belief system said God is not good, it affected everything else I did or even prayed for. If we believe things about God that aren't true, we are laying a faulty foundation for our lives that will sooner or later crack. If we have wrong thinking about God, we will have wrong thinking about everything else and wrong thinking leads to wrongdoing. Why? Because *what we believe about God ultimately determines the way that we live.*

Now, most of us don't consciously believe that God is not really good. And if we do feel it, we would never dare to say out loud "God is not really good" because, you know, theologically we know better. We know in our heads that God is good. And I believe that deep in many of our hearts there is this lurking suspicion that: *Yes, God may be good to everybody else, but God has not been good to me.* This lie is at the core of much of our wrong thinking about God.

Let me send you back to Genesis chapter one. Look at what God made and then see the description. Everything God made was good. Of course it was because it was a reflection of a good God. But when Satan wanted to tempt the woman to rebel against God, he planted in her mind the seed of doubt about God's goodness.

We doubt the goodness of God when we look at our personal lives and when we look at worldwide calamities or events. For instance, through the ministry I have with women at Center for Emerging Female Leadership, I've heard single women doubting the goodness of God because God has not brought them the husband that they're longing for. That's doubt on a personal level. But I've also heard doubt about the goodness of God in light of national or world events such as the Holocaust, famine in Ethiopia, or the massacre of students at Newtown, Connecticut or at movie theater in Colorado. How could God let evil like that happen? You know, when you have a sick child and your child gets well, it's like God is so good. He healed my child. Well, that's true. God is good. And he did heal your child. But can you still look up into the eyes of God when your eyes are filled with tears and your child doesn't get healed and say, "God is still good?" Our perspective is so that we cannot see and know what God sees and God knows.

I remember my husband preaching a message a while back through his tears as he talked about DJ (he's a constant sermon illustration for us) and he said, "Even if God never heals him, *God is good*. We don't serve God for loaves and fishes, we serve him because He is worthy of our devotion."

It took me a long time to be able to sing songs like "Lord You Are Good." When the worship was focused on the goodness of God during that painful time in my life, I mouthed the words. I couldn't sing them. I just didn't feel they were true.

I now know and believe without a shadow of a doubt now that MY GOD IS GOOD!

GOD IS JUST LIKE MY FATHER

For some of you, this won't be an issue because you had a great earthly father. But it was an issue with me because I didn't. My father as I mentioned elsewhere, walked out on my mom and me when I was just two years old. He was a drunken barber by day and a preacher by night. Basically a hypocrite. Although I have no recollection of him whatsoever, I had papa pains, daddy issues, father abandonment problems, whatever you want to call it. I didn't even realize it until I was married and on one Father's Day I just started to cry. I was trying to hold it in but I couldn't. I was almost embarrassed that in my thirties I was having pain in my heart due to my dad not being around. Yes, it all came out after a particularly good preaching on a Father's Day and I realized I had put these issues so deep in me that I had seriously forgotten about them. Until that day. My father walked out on me.

He wasn't there for me on the good *or* the bad days. He was absent. He didn't walk me down the aisle. He wasn't there for my children to have a grandfather. He didn't attend my graduations. He just wasn't around.

His lack of presence was glaring. I could not get when people said *God is like your father* because I felt it was horribly ignorant of them not to mention the fact that with so many fatherless kids in the world, a little side note reminding us kids that God wouldn't be like this father would have helped a great deal. Especially since according to Focus on the Family, the United States leads the world in fatherless families, with roughly 24 million children (or 34 percent of all kids in the United States) living in homes where the father does not reside. So do you get me? To this day I have never met, seen, nor heard from him. Stage set.

One of the purposes of God's revelation to believers as Father, I think, has to do with his revelation of being personal. Granted, this is by no means the only purpose of it, but I think it flows. Certainly, it is over and against the impersonal god of Islam, and the distant god of Gnosticism, and so with other various pagan gods. This was always a strange idea to me — a relationship to God as his daughter (albeit an adopted one). Let's face it. I had no idea what that meant or looked like 'cause I never had a father relationship. But I did learn to cling to a scripture, Psalm 68:5 "A father to the fatherless..."

All of this, of course, is simply the battle I've fought with trying to understand who God says He is. I can't speak for all those who have lost or never met their fathers. It is, though, what it is. And for now, I cling to the promise that He is a father to the fatherless, while I continue working out what exactly that means.

•

Our perception of God is affected — positively or negatively — by the men in our lives, especially the one who is supposed to be the main one... our father. You may not have had a dad walk out on you but you may have had a dad who was abusive, harsh, emotionally distant, and unable to express love. If that is the case, you may have also cringed when people would preach/teach that God is like your father. Like me, if you heard that, it didn't compute. Your BS caused you to believe the lie that our heavenly Father has the same frailties, failings, and faults as our imperfect earthly fathers.

GOD IS NOT ALL-POWERFUL

Look around you and see how vast this universe is that God has made. God is truly all powerful. The power of God is amazing and it has always been a wonder to me. I often look at the clouds and the sky and am just amazed by God's power. The Bible gives some great descriptions and verses about God's great power. Yet, when I went through my crisis with my son, after having what felt like *everyone* in the whole world that knew me, pray with him, and we still walked out of that hospital with DJ not healed, I felt God was not as powerful as I had heard and read He was. I was never able to articulate this belief as well as a very close friend who shared that when she went through some difficult times in her life, she viewed God as a superhero and like most superheroes they have at least one weakness. She saw God like Superman, who got hit with kryptonite.

So, of course, I took a liking to that analogy because that is exactly how I felt. The Omnipotence of the God I was serving was being called into question. God seemed not to have been able to do the one thing I asked, heal my son. So my BS allowed me to believe the lie that God just didn't have the power.

My belief system changed when I realized that the

answer lies in a proper understanding of God's omnipotence. Omnipotence does not mean God cannot exercise self-limitation. When we speak of God being omnipotent or all-powerful we must understand exactly what that means. It means that God is able to do anything that is consistent with His holy character and overall purpose for my life. Once I accepted and truly understood this, it helped me to change my belief system to truly believe that my God IS all-powerful and does not have a weakness. Now understand, I still don't like this truth. I wanted God to heal my son. Period. Caso cerrado. BUT because it is in His Holy character to want to heal, to be able to heal, that possibility is not moot. But I still have to love Him and believe in His power to do anything within his character, even if he doesn't do another single thing for me. The fact that He sent His Son to die on the cross for MY sins, should be enough.

If you notice, most of these beliefs were rooted in my desire for God to do something. To fix my problems. This way of thinking is deceptive because 1) God is not a genie God who exists to do whatever we tell Him to do and 2) it suggests that our existence in life is supposed to be pain free.

Max Lucado once shared that we have become conditioned to think we shouldn't have problems or if something is wrong, it should be fixed instantly. We can see that in the following scenarios:
• If you have a headache? Take Tylenol.
• If you can't sleep? Take a sleep aid.
• Don't like your boss? Quit and get another job.
• Don't like your church's preaching? Find another church.
• Men don't notice you? Dress like a hoochie and watch the power of attraction.
• And the list goes on.

Christianity for me at that time, and for many others right now, was nothing more than another way to get our problems fixed. We figured pray and believe and ye shall receive. You'll have money in the bank. Your friend will be cured of cancer. That man you've been waiting for will come walking through your door any minute. Your marriage will be salvaged, and all will be well in your world.

When we buy into these lies that all lead to the thinking that God should fix our problems, we end up angry, bitter, and frustrated with life.

But I didn't just believe lies about God. I believed lies about myself — one very big one, in fact. Maybe you'll find a bit of yourself in this lie as well, so you can reject it and find the truth of who God has made you to be. Check out the lie about myself:

I AM NOT WORTH ANYTHING

When I was told I had the mark of a "prostitute" in my teen years by the church's pastor, that left a mark in my spirit that made me believe I was not worth anything. After all, a prostitute? How low could he go in the labeling department? So many of the moms felt that I was a bad influence and that their sons shouldn't get serious with me. Most of them didn't have a clue who I was, yet they judged me. In fact, many of their own children were engaging in sex and other ill-advised behavior. Sure, I had made the mistake of allowing a boy to nibble at my neck, but that's it. I was as far away from a prostitute as I could be — I was a virgin. Yet I felt dirty, under the label the pastor gave me. I believed what the label meant and spent years feeling as if I had no value.

That label and yes, lie was imprinted in my memory bank and it led to the progression of my belief system that I wasn't worth much and actually made me very driven to always have something to prove to people.

What we believe about ourselves determines how we live. If we believe and act on lies, we will end up in a "situation of captivity," a bondage that can only be broken by the truth of God's word. This lie is one that I think most women deal with as well because most are seeking affirmation for a variety of reasons and thus, seek to gain approval of others. For me, I was driven to prove everyone wrong. So I set out to be better than their kids. Smarter, more involved in Kingdom things, like teaching, preaching, writing, and generally MORE of everything. Boy, was I exhausted. It was in my thirties that I stopped the merry-go-round and realized what was driving me was the negativity of my teen years. When you buy the lie that you are worthless no amount of affirmation is enough. As a matter of fact, you don't even believe people when they tell you something good about yourself because all you hear are the voices that said the opposite. This is because we let others determine our worth.

There is a great scripture that reminded me that Jesus too was rejected in a big way but *God chose Him anyway.* What determined His value was what God did. God chose Him and that is what made Him precious and determined what His value was... that scripture is: "As you come to him, the living Stone — rejected by humans but chosen by God and precious to him" — 1 Peter 2:4.

Once there was a preacher who shared this illustration; and I think it puts this in prescriptive for us:

If someone threw a masterpiece in the trash because he did not recognize or appreciate the fine art, would that make the painting any less valuable? Not at all. The one who knows how to spot treasure, the fine art collector, would spot the painting and say "that is a priceless piece, and I am willing to pay any price to acquire it." That is exactly what God did for you and me. He sent His Son Jesus to bear the cross for us because He declared we are worth it! Not worthless! He put a price tag on us and declared our soul to be of great value.

So I asked myself a question when I was 31: Whose opinion will I accept? Believing a lie will put you in captivity.

Believe the truth: You are priceless. That knowledge will set you free. It sure did for me!

Sometimes, we buy the lies about those around us. When we buy these lies, this compromises our relationships and stunts our growth. Check out this lie about others we often believe.

NO ONE CAN BE TRUSTED

Again, I am sharing the lies I bought into but as you read along in each category, you will notice you either resonate with the lie I bought into or you can make up a list of your own. But this lie is one that I still work on to this day. I have found that while all people can't be trusted, *some can be*. I started working on this particular belief system also in my 30's when the situation of my marriage crisis got out to most of the church I attended. This was after I spoke to one of the church gossips (who knew about the matter because her husband worked with my husband and was the one who told me about the entire thing) and I basically begged her not to say anything and she promised she wouldn't. I think it was about 48 hours later, that the vine was buzzing already about my marriage crisis. To say I was hurt was an understatement. The betrayal reinforced the BS that had taken root earlier in my life, that people could not be trusted.

As much as we would like for it to be true, the church does not consist of only safe people. If we are going to have a biblical view of relationships and people, we must see the church as God describes it. Our faith must be able to square with the reality of life as we find it *and* with the reality the Bible describes to us. Let's look at those two realities.

Even in the body of Christ, we find some harsh realities: judgment, pride, self-centeredness, manipulation, abandonment, abuse, control, perfectionism, domination, and every kind of relational sin known to humankind. The walls of the church do not make it safe from sin. In fact, the church by definition is composed of sinners.

To further complicate matters, the church by its very nature as a family of God activates our most primitive and dependent longings because we want a perfect family. God designed the church to be our second family, and we often take into the church our longing for security and love that we take into our families of origin. And for some, as in their original family, the wish is not only disappointed — it can be crushed altogether. What are we to do with that reality?

David said in Psalm 101:6 (NCV) that we can look for the truthful people: "I will look for trustworthy people so I can live with them in the land..." But we are not by nature so discerning. We come into the church feeling and wishing, "Take care of me. I need you. I shouldn't have to first figure out who is safe and who is not. You should be good and trustworthy." We want things to be right and often they are not.

When one person abuses, breaks, or takes advantage of our trust, we judge the entire body because of that. But as with any other organization, family, or group, one person's behavior cannot speak for everyone's behavior. When we learn that one person's poor behavior does not mean everyone should not be trusted, then we can begin to heal.

In fact, the church can be a healing place where lives are transformed and where powerful love and healing can take place. I'm a pastor and I definitely believe that the body of Christ is still God's instrument for our healing and restoration (1 Peter 4:10; Ephesians 4:16). So, the question rings in our needy hearts: Is the church safe, or is it dangerous? The answer is, "It is both." Sometimes we are fortunate to find good relationships, and other times we run into disaster.

The sad thing is that our ideals for the church do not reflect biblical reality, either. We think that the Bible promises a church where we find only safe people. But the Bible says that the church is full of wolves as well as sheep. In the church, we will find both healing and hurt. If we are going to find healing and minimize hurt we need to make sure that we see the church as God describes it to us. We need to operate according to biblical reality instead of our fantasized wishes.

In describing reality of the kingdom of God, Jesus told a story:

"The Kingdom of Heaven is like a farmer who planted good seed in his field. But that night as everyone slept, his enemy came and planted weeds among the wheat. When the crop began to grow and produce grain, the weeds also grew. The farmer's servants came and told him, 'Sir, the field where you planted that good seed is full of weeds!' 'An enemy has done it!' the farmer exclaimed. 'Shall we pull out the weeds?' they asked. He replied, 'No, you'll hurt the wheat if you do. *Let both grow together until the harvest.* Then I will tell the harvesters to sort out the weeds and burn them and to put the wheat in the barn.'" (Matthew 13:14-30, italics mine)

As this story shows, God allows unsafe people to be in the church. They are wolves in sheep's clothing, and they are dangerous. While they may seem religious, they may not even be true believers. While they do many things in His name, they are not His sheep. (Matthew 7:22-23).

So all this to say? Learn to discern! No not everyone can be trusted but some can be. The enemy wants you to be a loner because he knows that a loner will lose in the end. The way you become a loner is when you live by the lie that no one can be trusted. There are a lot of people who feel self-sufficient. Self-sufficiency is nothing more than a lie from the devil. The devil wants to isolate you in order to eat away at you in your thoughts. One night, I was watching the National Geographic Channel, and I saw a lion attacking some animals. The lion seemed to be actually aiming at a special one (quite likely the weakest — the ones that were dropping back, and the loners). He passed by some of the strong ones. He did not touch them — they seemed to be too much trouble to handle and he seemed to be seeking the easiest way to get his meal. He is after that loner — that one that is dropping back. Whenever you are a loner, you are setting yourself up to be eaten by Satan. Whenever you withdraw from the assembling of yourselves together, you are setting up yourself to be destroyed (Hebrews 10:25). This, my friends, is why loners lose in the end.

We need to qualify the above statement: the key word is *"yourselves."* You cannot assemble with people who are not walking in the truth, as the Lord shows it to you. God's promise is that if anyone earnestly desires the truth, that the responsibility or onus is upon God to lead him/her to the truth. Therefore, if your heart is not satisfied with a fellowship, you should either find where God wants you to be, or find people around you to speak to about God. Sometimes He will allow you to be in a desert, because He wants you to allow the living waters in you to flow and make an oasis in that desert. The excuse of many is that they have nobody to fellowship with — because of a variety of reasons, including lack of trust. This is not always true, because if God puts you in a wilderness, you will find that there are others out in the wilderness like yourself, and if your heart cries out to God, the Holy Ghost will bring you together.

Sometimes, the lies we tell ourselves are the biggest problem. Let's explore them.

ONE TIME WON'T HURT!

How many times have we been caught by this lie? Have we used this lie to justify our first drink, our first smoke (cigarettes or marijuana), drugs, etc.? Of course, when people first engage in those sins, it is always justified by saying, "It is just this once." How many times has "just this once" turned into two or three times, and ultimately a lifetime of practicing what we said we would do only "one time?"

If any are so foolish as to think that "one time won't hurt!" just ask David if his "one time" of fornication with Bathsheba was worth the loss of his sons, the rebellion of his children, and running from his enemies (I Samuel 11 to the end of his life). Ask Eve what she thinks of the lie, "one time won't hurt!" (Gen. 3). Ask people today whose lives have been ruined because of a "one time" sin if it was worth it, and if that "one time" sin did not hurt! Friends, this lie has been told over and over, and people continue to fall for it. Don't you do it!

NOBODY WILL EVER KNOW!

This is a lie for several reasons. First of all, when you sin, at least one person knows — you! Of course, if others are involved in a sin (they usually are when they assure you "no one else will know"), then they are going to know, too! Besides all this, one more important than all others will know about the sin, God! "The LORD's eyes see everything; he watches both evil and good people " (Prov. 15:3 NCV).

Jesus told His disciples that when they pray, give donations, or fast, to do so in a private manner, because He said "Your giving should be done in secret. Your Father can see what is done in secret, and he will reward you." (Matt. 6:4 NCV).

One day, we are going to be judged by God who sees all and will judge the *"secret things"* we have done (Ecc. 12:13-14; Rom. 2:16; II Cor. 5:10). He knows!

YOU CAN REPENT LATER

Who is it among God's creation that is promised a "later?" The Bible says *"now"* is the day of salvation (II Cor. 6:2), and "today, if you will hear His voice, do not harden your hearts as in the rebellion" (Heb. 3: 15 NKJV). Jesus said, "Do you not say, 'There are still four months and *then* comes the harvest'? Behold, I say to you, lift up your eyes and look at the fields, for they are already white for harvest!" (Jn. 4:35 NKJV). Who is promised a "later?" This is another of Satan's lies.

We know that the obituary page is filled with people who thought they had a "later" to make their lives right. The truth is, we don't! Seeing that all we have is "now," we need to take advantage of our opportunities in this life and become Christian while we can. (Mk. 16:16). Ananias emphasized this when he asked Paul, *"why are you waiting? Arise and be baptized..."* (Acts 22:16, NKJV). The only reason you have been blessed with this day is because God wants you to make your life right with him before it is too late (II Pet. 3:9)!

YOU DESERVE IT

Many have turned their backs on God because of what they thought they "deserved." Satan was able to deceive Eve because she thought she was not getting something from God that she "deserved" (Gen. 3:4-5). Adam soon followed. A host of sins are committed today because people think that they didn't get what they "deserved." The truth of the matter is **we ought to be thankful that we do not get what we deserve!**

What do we deserve? We deserve separation from God because of our sins (Isa. 59:1-2), not His fellowship (II Jn. 9). We deserve God's wrath (Rom. 3:23), not His mercy (Jn.

3:16). We deserve dying in our sins, not Jesus Christ dying for our sins (Matt. 20:28; II Cor. 5:21). Let us NEVER get so high-minded that we think that what we have received from God is what we deserve!

IT IS FOR A GOOD CAUSE

How many times have we heard this lie? No, the end does not justify the means! Sin is still sin no matter what the reason! One of Satan's most potent lies is to get man to justify his sin by looking for a possible "good side." The Bible teaches that some were punished though they were doing things for a supposed "good cause."

God put Uzzah to death because he had placed his hand on the ark and steadied it when the ox stumbled (II Sam. 6:6-7). Why was God's anger *"kindled against Uzzah?"* Because he was not authorized to touch the ark. "But," some may ask, "wasn't it a *good thing* for Uzzah to steady the ark?" Maybe, but he still was not authorized to touch the ark. In Paul's day, he told the Romans that some had *"**slanderously** reported"* that he had said, *"let us do evil, that good may come"* (Rom. 3:8 NKJV). Paul never said that, and it is wrong for us to teach this blasphemous doctrine. The end **does not** justify the means! As you read and study the Bible, you find that so far as God is concerned, the "getting there" is as important as the "goal." In other words, when God lays out a pattern or plan, He expects it to be followed to the letter. Noah understood this (Gen. 6:22). God told the Israelites that when it came to building the Tabernacle, *"See... that thou make all things according to the pattern..."* (Heb. 8:5 NKJV). We are not at liberty to devise our own plans, so long as the "goal" is accomplished!

Unfortunately, many have used reasoning like this to justify their sin and error. How many times have we heard people declare that what they were doing was a "good work" and therefore, God must be pleased and men ought to accept it? We need to learn and learn well that regardless of what might be accomplished, if God says it is a sin, we need to leave it alone.

THERE ARE OTHERS DOING WORSE!

How many times have we heard this? Perhaps our children have said this to excuse their behavior. Did you accept it from them? Of course, not! Would we accept this excuse in any other walk of life? No! Then why would we expect God to accept this excuse? How foolish! While we may categorize sin, God does not do that. He says, *"The soul that sinneth, it shall die"* (Ezek. 18:20). He says that our sin will separate us from Him regardless of the "size" of the sin, and regardless of whether others are doing worse (Isa. 59:1-2)! Remember King Omri? We read about him in I Kings 16:23-26. The Bible records that he was the most sinful king of all in the history of Israel. Did Omri's sins justify Jeroboam and the other kings who were "not as evil" as Omri? Of course not! Looking to others and seeing if they are worse than us is not a wise comparison (II Cor. 10:12).

Our standard today is the Word of God. We must speak by the Word of God (I Pet. 4:11). It will make us perfect (II Tim. 3:16-17), allow us to grow (I Pet. 2:2; Heb. 5:12-14), and one day it will be our standard in the judgment (Jn. 12:48). The Bible reveals that we will be judged on our own merits (Ecc. 12:13-14), not on what someone else has or has not done that makes us look better! Let us not fall for a lie that we would not accept from anyone else.

IT DOES NOT BOTHER MY CONSCIENCE

"Let your conscience be your guide" is the advice of many when faced with a questionable situation. While this can be good advice, it is not foolproof. The conscience can be trained not to bother you when you sin. The Bible tells us that our conscience can be *"seared"* (I Tim. 4:1-2) or *"defiled"* (Tit. 1:15-16). What this means is that even though you were brought up knowing right from wrong, your conscience will no longer bother you when you sin. Does this sound familiar? Consider the *"defiled"* conscience. Would this type of conscience be a very good guide?

Before he became a Christian, Paul was with those who stoned Stephen and consented to his death (Acts 7:58, 8:1). Paul found Christians and put them in prison for being Christians (Acts 8:3). He went to Damascus to obtain more authority to persecute the Christians in Acts 9:1-2. He declared that he wasted the church and was more zealous than his fathers in doing so (Gal. 1:13-14). Then, as Paul looked back on his life, he said, *"Men and brethren, I have lived in all **good conscience** before God until this day"* (Acts 23:1). Did Paul's conscience bother him as he consented to the death of Stephen, or as he took men and women and tried to get them to blaspheme the name of the Savior (Acts 26:11)? No! Therefore, we can see that our conscience cannot be the standard for judging right from wrong in every situation.

Please understand that when we sin, we will be held accountable regardless of whether or not it bothers our conscience. Let us only follow God's Word as our standard of authority. When we justify ourselves by our conscience, we are falling for one of the devil's lies!

WHAT IS THE TRUTH?

The truth is that we have not outgrown the Bible, and we still have a lot to learn if we are going to stop being fooled by the same lies that have been told since the beginning of time. The only way we will be able to keep from falling for the devil's lies is to immerse ourselves in the Truth (Jn. 17:17; Ps. 119:2-3, 9, 11).

James said, "Submit yourselves, then, to God. Resist the devil, and he will flee from you." (Jas. 4:7 NIV). Let us be like Christ who refused the devil and his lies on every occasion (Matt. 4:1-11; Lk. 4:1-13; I Pet. 2:21-22).

Satan is called the *"father of lies"* for a reason (Jn. 8:44 NIV). Over the years, the devil's tactics have not changed. Have you ever thought about why Satan uses the same lies over and over again to tempt us? He does this because they are effective. However, we can make his tools of none effect if we will turn to God in loving faith and obedience and follow His word. What will you do? Will you buy the lie again?

MAKE IT PERSONAL

1. What lies have you believed about God?
2. What lies have you believed about yourself?
3. What lies have you believed about others?
4. How has believing in those lies manifested itself in the way you live (i.e. make decisions, attitude, actions)?
5. Agree with God. After you list the lie (s) you have believed, find the scripture that agrees with God and is a fact to replace your ungodly BS.
6. Renew your mind (your thinking) by the Word of God. Read the following scriptures. What do these verses reveal about how God views you?
Psalm 139:13-18
Ephesians 1:3-8

Romans 5:6-8

EXERCISE: Evaluate the negative belief systems you have been writing about in this book. Are you starting to feel more empowered to change some of them? Why or why not?

_____

_____

_____

CHAPTER 7

BE AUTHENTIC

So far we have learned about the father of lies, when we bought the lie, and why we continue to buy the lie. I've even shared some of the lies I bought into, knowing you may find you've bought into the same. Now we begin to dive into how we can start to eradicate the lies that have stockpiled our belief systems with ungodly beliefs. The first move you have to make to do that is to be authentic. People seek authenticity, but what does "being authentic" mean? It's being real, not trying to fake it. Young people have the uncanny ability to smell phoniness from a mile away. If you are not for real, forget it. They have no use for you.

A lot of people who go to church *resemble* Christians, but they lack real authenticity. They have no living, vital relationship with Jesus Christ. The starting point of being an authentic Christian is being able to trust in God. We learn how to commit things to Him in prayer, and we find He is faithful to respond to our prayers. Trust is not always easy. Especially when we have ungodly beliefs stored up in our hearts and minds.

It is like the story of the man who pushed a wheelbarrow across a tight wire stretched over Niagara Falls. It was one thing for observers to say they trusted he could do it; it would be a different matter for them to volunteer to crawl into the wheelbarrow! Really trusting God means crawling into the wheelbarrow. I think when we first come to the Lord our relationship with Him is so fresh and vital that it is easier to trust Him. But we need to learn that a true trusting relationship with God grows stronger as we allow the Holy Spirit to play His role in our lives, along with the role we play in trust.

Solomon said, "Trust in the Lord with all thine heart; and lean not unto thine own understanding. In all thy ways acknowledge him, and he shall direct thy paths" (Proverbs 3:5,6, KJV).

There is the part we play: We trust in the Lord; and there

is the part He plays: He directs our path. Involved in trusting God is being a trustworthy person. The authentic Christian not only trusts God, but he is someone who is worthy of the trust of God's people.

AUTHENTIC CHRISTIANS ARE TRANSPARENT

If you have been in the church very long, you know there are people who are evasive and others who are downright deceptive. And there are those who are in denial; they have issues in their lives and their relationships that they never acknowledge or deal with. These are the kinds of people who often are the source of division and confusion.

Authentic Christians are transparent. What you see is what you get with them. They have learned through hard experiences that the transparent life is more likely to bring them the joy and peace of the Kingdom, so they are honest with themselves and with a close few about what is happening in their own lives and they are honest about issues they have with other people.

Transparent people learn the wisdom of living according to John's plea that we be transparent in our relationship with God, with ourselves, and with other people (1 John 1:7-9). That is, we live in confession of our sins, we find forgiveness of our sins, and we walk in truth and light with God and with others.

AUTHENTIC CHRISTIANS KNOW THEIR BS

Authentic Christians are not afraid to take a good look at themselves, practice the discipline of self-reflection, and allow the Holy Spirit to tell them the areas they need to work on. WYSIWYG is a term most computer veterans know the meaning of. When you work on a keyboard and then print what you have written or developed, you will get on paper what you see on the screen. That sentence expresses succinctly what most people expect when they associate with others, especially their leaders: *They want to get what they see* — the real person, not some role-playing individual, who hides their true identity behind a consciously or subconsciously constructed mask.

Christians have not always had a good reputation when it comes to authenticity. For some people, the word *Christian* is virtually synonymous with hypocrisy. The church, they say, may look pretty good on the outside, but inside, it is not trustworthy. Something like the products one can buy from street-smart vendors: expensive watches for very little money. I know people who love to shop in the "everything fake capital of the world" Chinatown in NYC! ME? I prefer the real thing even if it costs much more. It's real or nothing for me. In personal items and in personal life.

When things prove to not be genuine, this can be a serious matter. Producing and selling fake products may easily land people in court. But an even far more serious consequence than producing and selling fake products comes when those who profess to be Christians turn out to be fake.

As a committed Christian, pastor, and leader, I often ask myself whether the religion of people I see, meet, or hear about, is real. For instance, what are we to think about some of our politicians who emphasize, time and again, that they are born-again Christians while many of their actions do not demonstrate Christian values? Bringing it closer to home: many pastors and church leaders can tell you of instances where the most pious -appearing church members are the ones who hide many of their past acts, let alone their current ones! Older people, always criticizing the young for their behavior, conveniently forget their own far-from-perfect conduct. Judging others becomes a dangerous business.

When we do so, as Christ reminded us, we are likely to be oblivious of a serious plank in our eye while worrying about tiny specks in the eyes of others (Matt 7:3)

When people look at you, especially if you are a leader, what do they expect to see? Not someone totally perfect, but someone they can respect. They do not expect that we never make mistakes, never have occasional lapses of good judgment, and never have personal failures. They do not expect to meet someone who knows everything or has an instant solution for every problem. They do not even expect to deal with those who never have any doubts and are always absolutely sure about everything they believe. *But they do expect us to be real and authentic.* If we want to be listened to, and hope to have our leadership role recognized, if we want to bring the gospel to a non-churched audience, and if we seriously try to relate to secular people — inside and outside of our own congregations — we must be authentic. Otherwise, however hard we try, we will not connect.

Personally, an area God continuously has to help me with is dealing with people around me who are as fake as fake can come. I sometimes feel like I want to have a Tourette syndrome outbreak and just say "you're fake" but of course, proper protocol disallows such behavior. However, I'm being authentic when I say, it's hard for me to associate on a close personal level with people I feel are fake. Pray for me.

Now, if you are reading this book and really want to eradicate the lies that have been rooted in your BS for as long as you can remember, you need to be authentic with yourself and with God. There is no way *anything* will be able to help you until you are honest that you have some seriously ungodly BS inside of you.

With that said, what are the main ingredients for authenticity? No detailed, strategic plan exists that, if carefully executed, will transform us from someone who mostly plays a role and hides behinds a mask into a transparent, open, and genuinely authentic person. But here are several elements that can help us become real and authentic.

1. **Be honest.** If we want to be authentic, we must learn to be honest with ourselves and others, in particular about who we are and what happens in our own lives. Some of us are extremely clever in hiding who we are deep down, and often we have become quite skillful in running a constant public relations campaign for ourselves. The actuality of our life may, however, differ quite sharply from the image of ourselves that we seek to promote.

The truth may remain hidden for a long time. The sad reality remains that some people who faithfully attend church — even very active people — do not have a meaningful, personal spiritual life. Some may claim to be Christians but secretly cheat on their spouses. Some may be church elders but do not return a faithful tithe. Research shows that there are pastors who seldom read the Bible and pray outside of their professional engagements. But, sooner or later, it will show. And, whether we like it or not, there are people around us who have an uncanny ability to smell that something does not add up.

Be sure to pursue honesty. Take a personal inventory, do the exercises in this book and list the BS that has controlled your life up until this point and if you do not like what you see, then pray and allow God to change your life. It may require a few confessions. It may require asking for forgiveness — from God as well as from fellow human beings. It will certainly require you replacing ungodly BS with godly ones. But being honest will lead you to be the person God created you to be and eventually lead you to your destiny and earn the respect of those you serve. Living a lie does not bring that respect — in the end it only brings disillusion.

2. **Acknowledge doubts.** Admitting that we, at times, have our doubts does not undermine our role as a parent, leader, or minister. Those who say they never have had any

doubts either never do some hard thinking or are fooling themselves and others. Every Christian, including pastors, will at times have to deal with doubt. The question focuses not so much on whether we have doubts, but on what we do with them. Do we cherish the doubts and claim that our doubts are the result of our superior intelligence? Or do we search for more depth? Do we struggle with our questions, one by one, and read, talk, and pray to find answers?

3. **Face vulnerability.** To always talk about ourselves would be wrong. After all, what we have to say in our role as a Christian is not just about us. Yet, we should be open about ourselves and make no secret not only of the things that have gone well in our lives, but also of the things that did not go so well or of moments when we failed. When my husband and I get the opportunity to teach or preach, we always share our personal stories as they relate to the message. It took me some time to learn this, but I have discovered that many people are more inclined to hear me when they sense that they are connecting with someone who knows from her own experience what she is talking about. This builds their willingness to communicate with me when they sense that I am no stranger to many of the things with which they are currently struggling. The hardest thing to do for many people is to connect to someone they feel has no clue of what is happening in the real world around them.

4. **Listen to the stories of others.** I've learned that everybody has a story. While I find it hard sometimes to take time to listen to the stories of others due to the busyness of life, I realize that people today are looking for someone to listen. Television viewers want to see the people behind the news; they want to know more about famous people and royalty. Newspapers and journals abound with interviews and news about people. Often the method of gathering this information goes far beyond what we consider acceptable, but this is what sells.

People want to see a picture of the real us, and — within limits — they have a right to have this. But never forget that people are just as eager to tell their own story to you. People today may reject grand stories but they embrace small, local personal stories. Real relationships do not come about until personal stories are told about who you really are and who the people you connect with really are.

One way to do this is to get involved with book clubs that do books that stretch you. I'm not talking about books that are novels, to me that is a waste of time. Books that challenge you by making you think about why you believe what you believe and make you reflect on the person you are becoming with a group of like-minded women always help you become a more authentic self. I have done this for the last few years and I have always been impacted by them.

5. **Act authentically**. Far more people are interested in knowing that we are quality individuals — people who have a genuine interest in who they are and what they feel, rather than in hearing our views on all kinds of theological minutiae. Most people consider it far more important that we are honest people who live up to the promises we make than to be assured that we understand all doctrinal interpretations. Have you ever been around some people who all they want to do is show you have well-read they are, how extensive their vocabulary is and basically how smart they are? This does not say that doctrinal beliefs are unimportant, but we cannot overemphasize the enormous shift that has taken place in the minds of many church members and non-churched people alike. Before they will listen to us, they must be convinced that we are real.

The ultimate litmus test in today's world is not whether the things I preach are biblically true and defendable, but whether the people I work for and with whom I associate see that the things I proclaim and promote have become a concrete reality in my own life. Has my faith clearly changed the priorities in my daily life? Do people see that my life is real, that it matters?

When people around us look at us, what do they see? Someone who leads a real life and leaves a trail worth following and a story worth listening to? Do they see a faithful steward who always acts with integrity? A genuine disciple of the Lord Jesus Christ? A person who always attempts to relate to others in a truly Christian way? Someone who is transparent and can be trusted in every respect? Not just occasionally, when we have a good day, but 24/7?

CHRIST: THE ULTIMATE EXAMPLE OF AUTHENTICITY

Becoming authentic is a process that we can never complete — it will always remain a work in progress. We find complete authenticity only in Jesus Christ. He was who He was and is who He is. The process toward becoming authentic is, therefore, one of becoming more like Him. Paul urges us: "Your attitude should be the same that Christ Jesus had. Though he was God, he did not demand and cling to his rights as God. He made himself nothing; he took the humble position of a slave and appeared in human form" (Philippians 2:5-7, NLT).

What applies to us individually also applies to us as a faith community. The question is not limited to, Am I an authentic person? The question has a sequel: Is my church a community that radiates authenticity? Is it an open community that attracts people, because it clearly cares for people and lives up to what it professes to be? The church we serve does not become a truly authentic community simply by talking about or writing about it. Slogans by themselves are not sufficient.

Becoming authentic, individually and collectively, calls for a positive response to God's invitation. But if we are not authentic, no hope exists of genuinely connecting with the people we seek to serve. Our authenticity is an invitation for others to respond to God's call. Our journey to authenticity begins when we know the belief systems that we have and begin a journey to replace the lies the enemy has told us with the truth of God's word. Then and only then, can we be on our way to being spiritually healthy individuals because those kinds of people are authentic.

EXERCISE: How can you allow your authentic self to show? Write about that here.

_____

_____

_____

CHAPTER 8

SEE THE BEST IN YOURSELF

There is a song by Marvin Sapp that has been such a blessing to me. Perhaps you've heard it, it's called "The Best In Me" and it talks about how God saw the best in him when others did not. Boy does this song take me to a place of gratefulness! This song is a powerful declaration to the enemy that God only sees the best in me, what we were destined for, unlike many around us in church and society who see the worst in us. Who remember every mistake and can't believe God can transform our lives.

The challenge for us as believers who have been buying the lies of the enemy is that we can't see the best in ourselves. We know what we've done, what we've thought in our minds. We only hear the voices of those who have labeled us, condemned us, and ridiculed us. We don't see from God's perspective. We only see from the shady perspective of the enemy of our souls and those he's used in our lives to speak over us.

In order for you to work on eradicating the BS you have in you right now, formed because of the lie you have bought from Satan, you have to start seeing and believing in the best in you from God's perspective. Plus, you have to start doing the things that will keep affirming those belief systems.

How do you see yourself? Pause for a moment and think about it. What thoughts have you had about yourself today? As women, so many of us find ourselves:

• basing our self-worth on how others see us and on our accomplishments
• feeling shame from our past
• defining our value based on our looks
• setting unrealistic standards for ourselves

But it doesn't have to be this way. If only we could see ourselves as God sees us. He sees the BEST!

An angel of God appeared to Mary, announcing that she of all women would conceive a child, who would be called Jesus in Luke 1:26-38 NIV. Mary was at first astonished and confused about how this could happen when she had not been with a man, but when the angel explained that the Holy Spirit would give her the child, she accepted the prophesy and went on.

Mary was able to see in herself the beauty that God saw. He saw her as worthy of this great gift. God often blesses us in amazing ways, but so many times, we doubt if we are worth the gifts. We question God or wonder how He could pick us for those blessings — the gift of words, speaking, discernment, teaching, etc. May we be more like Mary and embrace God's vision of us.

Understanding how God sees us and how He values us can help us see the truth about ourselves. How we see ourselves and how we understand our place in the world has a profound impact on us. You could even say that it shapes the whole of our lives. As I mentioned before, this is why Satan will always introduce lies to us that distort what we think God thinks of us. But let me remind you how God sees you!

BEAUTIFUL YOU

Handcrafted by a loving Creator, you were etched from your toes to your head. You are not a mistake. Society may say you don't fit the beauty mold, but God looks at you and smiles, knowing that He created you just the way He wanted. Do you think God failed to get the latest fashion magazine to see if you fit today's view of what is beautiful? Over the decades our society's view of beauty has changed but God's has not.

"Before I formed you in the womb I knew you, before you were born I set you apart," the Word says in Jeremiah 1:5 NIV.

UNIQUE YOU

God is an artist and you are His canvas. All around us is the beauty God created, and it is the variations and uniqueness that set us apart. It would be pretty boring if everyone acted and looked the same.

"Does the clay say to the potter, 'What are you making?'" — *Isaiah 45:9 NIV*

"Indeed, the very hairs of your head are all numbered." — *Luke 12:7 NIV*

SO CHANGE THE WAY YOU SEE

I read a great quote on Facebook one day. It said, "Don't change the way you look. Change the way you see." No matter how much we try to alter our outside appearance it won't make us truly happy. The heart needs to be transformed, so we may begin to see ourselves and others through God's eyes. If we spent half as much time beautifying our inside as we do our outside we would be receiving a lot more joy and victory. I see so many women who worry about the latest brand name bag, cosmetics, dresses, etc. and don't even think twice about how they are being formed spiritually. I like those things myself but my priority has been and will always be my inside versus what I have on the outside.

"Charm is deceptive, and beauty is fleeting; but a woman who fears the LORD is to be praised." — *Proverbs 31:30 NIV*

WHAT DOES GOD SEE AS BEAUTIFUL?

You are God's masterpiece. If He wanted you to be designed another way He would have created you that way. Dwelling on what you don't like about your physical appearance or how you are wired (introvert vs. extrovert) probably isn't that pleasing to the One who created you.

Some days I think, yes, I am beautiful and I am pleased. Other days I think, no, not so much. Then I'm discouraged. Why? Well, to be honest, because sometimes I like what I see when I look in the mirror and other times I don't. The truth is though, the way God sees me doesn't change from day to day. Can we say hallelujah to that?!

Right now in my mismatched pajamas, God thinks I'm beautiful. Right now in my makeup-less face, God thinks I'm beautiful. Right now with pimples on my chin, and these dark spots on my forehead that are coming from nowhere as I age, God thinks I'm beautiful... and He thinks you are, too. God's view of us doesn't fluctuate with the number of pimples, volume of frizz, or amount of cellulite we have. We buy into these lies that so easily deceive. Can we finally start to see ourselves as God sees us, as His masterpieces, the best of creation? We need to start saying the truth that will replace the lies the enemy has told us:

I am God's child (Jn. 1:12 NIV). We are daughters of the Most High King, His princesses. We bear His image and share in His inheritance. We have been grafted into God's family; here we find belonging.

I have been bought with a price. I belong to God (1 Cor. 6:19,20 NIV). We have been given worth. We cost something. We cost Jesus' life and death. Our beauty flows out of our value and this value out of God's choice to transform our lives.

I have been redeemed and forgiven of all my sins (Col. 1:14 NIV). The ugliness of sin does not permanently scar our identities. We are redeemed from failure, guilt, and shame. When we can let go of our past, as well as our sin, we can begin to see ourselves as God sees us — beautifully.

I am complete in Christ (Col. 2:10 NIV). We are not inadequate. We are not lacking. We are not limited. We are women, made whole, in Christ.

I cannot be separated from the love of God (Rom. 8: 35 NIV). Nothing can strip us of God's love. We have nothing to fear on earth because God's love for us can withstand all things for all time.

I am God's workmanship (Eph. 2:10 NIV). We are God's masterpieces! We have been created with planning and purpose unique to each woman.

I am chosen of God, holy and dearly loved (Col. 3:12; 1 Thes. 1:4 NIV). We are wanted. Sometimes it seems hard to believe, but God wants us! He chose us, and He loves us beyond what we can imagine.

I died with Christ and died to the power of sin's rule over my life (Rom. 6:1-6 NIV). We do not have to believe Satan's lies any longer.

We are no longer bound to a definition of beauty that is measured in pounds and calories. We are no longer slaves to the opinions of others on our walk, talk, style, or swag! We are beautiful in our identity in Jesus Christ!

YOU ARE LOVED

Embrace the fact that you have a God that loves you personally. He did not compare you with His other creations but lovingly designed you. He looks past your mask of hurt and pain and sees His beloved child. You are beautiful! See the best in yourself and don't buy the lies of the enemy anymore. You are... fearfully and wonderfully made. (Psalm 139:14 NIV)

EXERCISE: You've just seen how beautiful God thinks you are. Now, let's make sure you believe it. Write a love letter from God — to you. Start with your name. "Dear Your Name ..."

_____

_____

_____

WATCH YOUR COMPANY

A side from God, I don't think I could have made it without the help and support of my friends. When I was a young girl, like many young girls I had what I thought were friends. Since I grew up in the church, they were mostly church girlfriends. But eventually jealously, cattiness, and backstabbing took its course and I vowed never to be close to women again. As a matter-of-fact, I always had way more friends who were boys than girls. I was the cool girl the guys asked for advice, who wasn't so prissy that I couldn't hang out on the park benches of the Lower East Side, and I was okay with that role. Girls wanted me to tell them how guys think and guys wanted me to tell them how girls think; I was so the go-to person!

For most of my high school and college life, I didn't really have girlfriends I could confide my innermost struggles. I just didn't trust them. I had been too hurt by them. However, almost as if God was preparing me for the storms that would eventually come hard in my life, he opened my heart to risk letting some women in and while it has been hard work to maintain these relationships (because anything worthwhile requires time investment), it has been the greatest thing I did "for myself." You see, a great way to keep your mind on track on your quest to eradicate the lies the enemy has fed you all these years is to surround yourself with Christian friends who are going to encourage you, pray with you, tell you God's truth, challenge you when you are buying a lie again, and lift your spirits when you need it!

"As iron sharpens iron, so one person sharpens another."
— *Proverbs 27:17 NIV*

•

Seems that I was on to something because while most people feel that many of our modern social problems, from divorce to homelessness and obesity, are often thought to be based in areas such as poverty, stress or unhappiness, some researchers suggest we are overlooking something crucial:

friendship. It would appear that our society is ignoring its importance, just as I did for so many years.

The philosopher Aristotle said, "In poverty and other misfortunes of life, true friends are a sure refuge. They keep the young out of mischief; they comfort and aid the old in their weakness, and they incite those in the prime of life to noble deeds." Friendships are vital for wellbeing, but they take time to develop and can't be artificially created. No wonder they are at risk of being neglected. Even now, as a bi-vocational executive pastor, mom, speaker through my ministry with the organization I founded Center For Emerging Female Leadership, director of Academic Operations at a college in Miami, and of course, wife to the most amazing husband, I still wonder how I will make time to hang out with friends. But I do it because I remember how crucial they have been to me in my life, especially when I was rebuilding my belief systems. When your belief systems are challenged — especially as you read this book and determine that you will work on them — you are going to need sister friends to help you along the way. But you can't expect friends to be in your winter when you haven't cultivated them in your spring.

Not any old person can be in your circle. You need people who are God-strong, who are not perfect, of course, but have belief systems that are God-based because if you don't watch your company, you end up being very much like them in various regards.

Tom Rath in his book, *Vital Friends: The People You Can't Afford To Live Without*, makes the point that if you ask people why they became homeless, why their marriage failed or why they overeat, they often say it is because of the poor quality, or nonexistence, of friendships. They felt outcast or unloved.

Rath undertook a massive study of friendship, alongside several leading researchers.[1]

---

[1] Tom Rath. Vital Friends: The People You Can't Afford To Live Without. Simon & Schuster. 2006.

His work resulted in some surprising statistics: If your best friend eats healthily, you are five times more likely to have a healthy diet yourself. Married people say friendship is more than five times as important as physical intimacy within marriage. Those who say they have no real friends at work have only a one in 12 chance of feeling engaged in their job. Conversely, if you have a "best friend at work," you are seven times more likely to feel engaged in your job. I remember when I first read this book, I said to myself no wonder the best job I ever felt I had (working at the Latino Pastoral Action Center) was because I worked with people I considered friends and to this day, many are still in my life! Two of my former staff members are my very best friends!

The book recommends carrying out your own "friendship audit," in order to recognize which of your friendships provide you with the different things you need, then to sharpen each friendship in line with its strength. Of course, it's not always a good idea to judge friends in a detached way, or to doubt a friendship just because you can't easily identify its rewards. The closest friends like each other for who they are in themselves, not for what they deliver. In fact, Aristotle made the point that it is better to give than to receive in friendship. Aristotle also believed that friendship can only arise indirectly, like happiness.

Friendships with other women have the potential to either enrich your life greatly or hurt you deeply. I've experienced both but you can navigate the complex dynamics of relationships well if you realize that God wants to use your friendships to help you and your friends grow. Grown-up friendships with like-minded women stretch and encourage both you and your friends to become more mature and strengthen Godly belief systems and can many times expose ungodly ones.

As you begin to work on who you are and what you believe and have believed that was erroneous, you will need spiritual friends. So what do spiritual friends look like? Any good friendship includes high levels of trust and intimacy. Most friends have shared interests and mutual enjoyment of one another.

But spiritual friendship adds another dimension. Spiritual friends help us pay attention to what's going on deep within us at a soul level, and they help us notice and pay attention to God and to His work in our lives. More than that, spiritual friends help us live within God's will. Spiritual friendships have the ability to restore life to our souls. Spiritual friends feel each other's pain and share each other's joy.

This is a special joining of hearts where lives are shared in a covenantal relationship that fosters the spiritual development of all parties involved, and where there is a greater awareness of and response to God's presence. It touches us at a soul level and opens us to greater levels of transformation, so that God's glory may be reflected in our lives.

My spiritual friends make me more aware of sinful behaviors in my own life — parts of me that don't look anything at all like Christ — and help me identify areas that need God's redemptive work. But they also remind me of my belovedness and help me notice the places where I do resemble Christ, where there is evidence of His transformation in my life. I weather stormy seasons of life better because they are with me. My celebrations are much richer because of the shared experience. Laughter comes easily as we notice and celebrate the joy of living in Christ. These friends help me offer and receive forgiveness. In the context of these friendships, I find that I am less burdened emotionally.

Spiritual friendships provide a level of intimacy that gives me a glimpse of what is shared within the Trinity, between Father, Son, and Holy Spirit. There is no agenda in these relationships, no "what can you do for me" thinking, no jockeying for position. No comparing of successes in church growth, academic credentials, or the achievement of our children. These kinds of friendships are marked by honesty, love, and acceptance. They help us discern God's will and the presence and leading of the Holy Spirit.

When we find ourselves in a spiritual desert or wilderness, when we are in that unstable place where we are trying to reinvent ourselves because the person we thought we were was based on lies that we bought from the enemy, when tragedy strikes and the bottom falls out, when our ministry or our marriage is failing, when our precious child becomes a prodigal and the disciplines that have held us in God's presence seem so lonely, we need to have friends, not let's have a party friends (although there will be a time for that), not let's go shopping friends (although shopping is great) no, we will need spiritual friends who will help us find our way in the darkness, help us get our feet back on solid ground, help us know where God is, help us discern Satan's lies and God's truth, and help us celebrate the grace in our lives.

I'm thankful for my spiritual friends. I'm more of who God wants me to be because of them. I have a close group of girlfriends that we call WEPA. It's a Puerto Rican slang term meaning wow, awesome, hey! But we have used it not only because we are all Puerto Rican (so far) but as an acronym to mean "women encouraging progressing advancing" each other. WEPA ladies are all very different not only in style but ideology yet we have found a way to support each other's dreams and be there for each other's disappointments.

The group started out with five but eventually dwindled to just three. Why? Because as has already been stated it takes time to build friendships and not everyone is willing to put in the time. One casually drifted off because of time and distance, the other because our times together were not only times of fun and casual talk but also actually challenges to grow, stretch and change. Many times we would read a book that would make us take a hard look at ourselves and we would help each other see areas about ourselves we didn't even know were there. Not everyone is ready for that kind of in- your-face growth challenge, so she faxed us a letter stating that her therapist felt it was best she leave the group.

Regardless of the many challenges WEPA has faced with each member of the group, we have made a promise to each other that we will grow old together. Obviously, not everyone stayed true to that promise but I still hold each one dear to my heart. For a time period, they were essential to my growth as I sorted out my BS as much as I was essential to theirs. For those of us who remain, we try to continue to do what we have done to challenge each other in the area of spirituality, belief systems, and theological reflection. We've even branched out to other women who fit the criteria for us of potential spiritual friends. This is crucial because if you don't watch your company, you can easily end up surrounded by people who will support the person you are not meant to be versus the one God wants you to be.

Friends have given me what I needed in the areas of acceptance, support, discipline, modeling, and a host of other relational ingredients that produce change. Good friendships are an absolute must for our spiritual growth to happen. In picking good friendships that produce growth, several qualities are important:

• Transparency and authenticity.
• Acceptance and grace.
• Mutual struggles, although they do not have to be the same ones.
• Loving confrontation.
• Familiarity with the growth process where both parties have "entered in" and have some knowledge of the process so as to avoid the blind leading the blind.
• Mutual interest and chemistry, a genuine liking.
• An absence of "one-up and one-down" dynamics.
• Both parties in a relationship with God.
• Honesty and reality instead of "over spiritualizing."
• An absence of controlling behavior.

• Both parties need other support systems as well to avoid the same kind of toxic dependency on each other that led to the problems.

That is what I found in my WEPA circle. I had never experienced it before and it was life changing. When I went through my marriage crisis and the life threatening operations with my youngest son, it was my friends' willingness and ability to handle my rants to God, my uncontrollable tears, my anger, and my confusion that ultimately showed me Christ with skin on. Maybe you should consider starting your own WEPA circle.

HOW DO YOU WATCH YOUR COMPANY

I would say a good way to watch your company is to watch and see if the people you continually hang out with have any of the following traits of unsafe people. If they do, they are not the ones you are looking for in spiritual friendships.

1. Unsafe people think they "have it all together" instead of admitting their weaknesses. James 5:16, Ecclesiastes 4:10. Their friends will:
a. Feel disconnected.
b. Feel "one down" or weaker than they actually are.
c. Feel dependent on the "strong" one while perhaps feeling anger and hostility about it.
d. Feel the need to compete to reverse the role.

2. Unsafe people are religious instead of having a right spirit. Luke 18:10-14
a. They do not identify with others as fellow sinners.
b. This sets up comparison, competitive strivings, defensiveness, and alienation.
c. They "project" onto others, unable to own their own

flaws.

3. Unsafe people are defensive instead of open to feedback. Proverbs 9:7-9, Matthew 18:15-17

4. Unsafe people only apologize instead of changing their behavior. Luke 3:7-9

5. Unsafe people:

a. Do not admit they have problems or think they can solve the problem themselves.

b. Do not confess when they have wronged someone.

c. Do not forgive people who have hurt them.

d. Avoid facing relationship problems directly and openly.

e. Do not hunger and thirst for righteousness.

f. Treat others with a lack of empathy.

g. Are not open to confrontation.

h. Are not in the process of learning and growing.

i. Blame other people for their problems.

j. Do not want to share their problems with others to help them grow.

6. Unsafe people demand trust, instead of earning it. John 10:37-38_

a. If we are truly trustworthy, we would welcome questioning of our "trustability."

b. If we are truly serious about growing, we want to know if we are doing something wrong. **Ps.139:23-24**

7. Unsafe people blame others instead of taking responsibility. Genesis 3:12-13

8. Unsafe people lie instead of telling the truth.

•

We are all deceivers to some degree. The difference between safe and unsafe liars is that safe people own their lies and see them as a problem to change as they become aware of their deception.

But let's say you haven't been able to create a circle of

Christian friends. Ask God to bring you even one friend who can walk with you and believe in you and He will. But you need to make yourself open to new friendship... you never know where or when you'll encounter the friend who will change your life! My WEPA girls and the new friends I've allowed in my life in the last few years have changed mine immensely!

EXERCISE: Write down the names of the two to five people you talk with, hang out with, or see the most. Then write down whether each of these people is a positive influence in your life and why.

_____

_____

_____

CHAPTER 10

MOVE ON IT

S o how can we change our beliefs? Before I give you the four steps that I have personally practiced in my life to get rid of bad BS, you must do the following to prepare yourself for a new mindset.

NOTICE

The first thing you must do is look at the decisions you've made in your life. Who have you become involved with? What is the quality of your love relationship? What is your work situation? Do you have enough money? Do you feel satisfied creatively? Do you have areas of your life that bring you joy? Are there areas of your life that you ignore or try not to notice? Take the time to *notice*. Our BS inevitably shows us pictures in our lives. If we just take the time to look, we can see everything we believe about ourselves, our worth, our position in the world, reflected in our lives. You might find it helpful to just make a list of all the things you observe, the things in your life that you're not happy with, and the beliefs you can detect there. Some examples:

I never have enough money. I must believe I don't deserve money. Or maybe I don't believe it's "right" and "loving" to have money in this world where so many people don't have enough. I'm afraid of being thought of as greedy and unloving.

I don't feel good about my body. I believe that when I'm overweight, nobody will love me. People will be repulsed by me if I become too fat. I hate the way I look; I hate myself.

Every time I try to speak to a group of people, I get rejected. Do I believe I deserve this? I believe I'm stupid and have nothing to say anybody would want to hear. I believe it's wrong (unloving) to want to speak my truth.

Notice that each belief is founded on a feeling — fear, self-hate, grief, pain, rage…

And the pain is covered by a judgment that says something is wrong, bad, not good enough, unloving... The judgment based on a lie from the enemy becomes a belief that carries into our lives.

SET YOUR MIND

This is a very powerful action. Setting an intention to change a belief is an act of will, and is tied strongly to your soul. It is powered by emotion. In other words, it is fueled by the desire to change, by wanting something new, something different. The intention usually starts with a statement that looks forward:
• I WILL change my life.
• I INTEND to have more love in my life.
• I WILL become a better person.
• I WILL believe God's Word in every area of my life!

LET IT GO

This action takes an erroneous belief and lets go of it. Releasing works well with very frozen judgments or beliefs, especially beliefs that encompass large parts of our lives, such as our basic worthiness. Releasing involves making formal statements of what we have believed, and usually begin with:
• I no longer believe... OR... I let go of the belief that... OR... I forgive myself for having believed that:
• I am unworthy
• I am unlovable
• I deserve to be poor/in danger/in a state of lack, etc.

Everyone who knows me knows that I am very big on ceremony. Perhaps you can create a ritual to document this next phase of your life such as writing your old BS down on slips of paper and burning them, or putting them on one 8½x11 paper and just tearing the paper up and throwing it away. But the important thing is that this step begins the shaking up process of letting go of your old BS and replacing it with new Godly BS.

AFFIRM THE NEW YOU

You've identified old beliefs and taken the step to let go of the old BS. Next, we begin the process of building a new set of beliefs. This is the action of Affirming. The word AFFIRM comes from the Latin word affirmare, which is to make firm. Webster's adds: VALIDATE, CONFIRM, to state positively, to assert or decree as valid or confirmed.

Letting go of the old is not enough. You must fill the space with something new. With this action, you begin the creation of a new template for your life. You begin the process of changing your decisions and beliefs. You MAKE FIRM a new set of decisions and beliefs.

An affirmation is a statement of present reality. It should be stated as a positive, not a negative, and as a present reality, not a future one. For instance:

YES	NO
I AM confident that I am God's child.	I am not a child of the King.
I have good, loving relationships.	I will be rid of people who don't appreciate me or don't value me.
I am worthy of being loved.	I don't deserve to be treated badly.

So much has been written on affirmations, and this tool has been embraced so heavily by the New Age community, that it has unfortunately become almost a joke. The difference here is that as believers we must base what we believe and "affirm" on the Word of God.

You will always have three choices in life:

1) Believe what others say about you.

2) Believe what you're "feeling" based on Satan's lies about you.

3) Believe what God's truth says about you.

•

If the ladder is not leaning against the right wall, every step we take just gets us to the wrong place faster. — Stephen R. Covey

•

There is no question that in life you have already been taking steps. Some backwards and some forward but no doubt you have been taking steps. But not all of those steps, whether they were in the physical or in the spiritual, were steps that took you to the right places — the places God ordained for you to be walking in right now.

EXERCISE: Write down three new belief systems you are ready to embrace as the result of reading this book. Discuss how these belief systems can help or enhance your life.

_____

_____

_____

CHAPTER 11

RETRAIN YOUR BRAIN

The only way you can replace ungodly BS with godly BS is to retrain your brain or what Romans 12:2 speaks of when it says be transformed by the renewal of your mind. I'm sharing what has worked for me in my life. When I thought I would die. NO when I *wanted* to die because of what I experienced I slowly, eventually went through the mind steps I've listed here and it helped me to retrain my brain from ungodly belief systems to godly ones... from a poverty mindset that could have kept me in the projects and out of education to the woman I am today. I still practice these steps when I am feeling the weight of life and when I go through my "nobody cares" moments. You don't have to practice them in any type of order but you will have moments when you have to revisit each of them. Doing these mind steps will help you get rid of bad BS and help you replace them with good ones. It will help you live the life you were meant to live, God's way because you won't be buying any more of the enemy's lies!

So let's jump in... here are my six steps to a new mindset that will help you never to buy a lie again!

1) RECALL

The first mind step is to recall what God brought you through already that you know you could not have survived without His supernatural help. Why is it so important to recall? Well, recalling helps to build your faith for the now, because God tells us He is the "very present help in time of trouble." It helps you see how you can trust God because you recall all the moments you know that you know that you know, it was GOD who helped you out!

In the middle of our mess, in the middle of our need, in the middle of our desperation we need to go back and remember, recall. We need to recall whose we are!

Yes, the state of our culture is horrifying. Our economy is in the pits and many of the things happening in our society have had a direct impact on us or people we know. But when we are down and out, when we feel that we can't keep going and our get-ups are over, that our life is not winning and our spirit is dying, we need to remember this first mind-step for a new mind-set: RECALL!

When we recall, we bring something back to mind. We remember. Lamentations 3:21-26 NIV says "Yet this I call to mind and therefore I have hope..."

In the Old Testament, God commanded His people to celebrate certain feasts so they would not forget what He had done for them, and so they could pass on those inspiring stories to the next generation. Several times a year, the Israelites stopped whatever they were doing and everybody celebrated how God brought them out of slavery, or how God defeated this enemy or how He protected them against that calamity. These celebrations were not optional. They were commanded and the people were required to attend and remember God's goodness to them.

In other places, the Bible records how God's people put down "memorial stones." These large markers were to remind the people of specific victories God had given them. Every time they or future generations passed by the memorial, they would remember the mighty things God had done. Do something similar. Take time to remember your victories, and celebrate what God has done in your life. Put out some memorial stones. Plan a "look what the Lord has done party," perhaps as an alternative to a secular-style New Year's Eve party. Or do it as a new way to celebrate a milestone birthday!

This is one of the best ways to build your faith and strengthen your new belief systems while keeping yourself encouraged. Yes, as the Word also tells us, "... But David *encouraged himself* in the Lord His God" (1 Samuel 30:6 KJV). Sometimes you have to encourage yourself! No, wait... *most* of the time, you have to encourage yourself! Recall the time that God made a way for you when it looked as if there was no way! Recall when you were so lonely and God brought somebody special into your life. Recall how God healed you or someone you know when the doctors said "start making funeral arrangements." Recall the time you got amazing strength and peace to deal with the passing of a loved one unexpectedly. Recall how He protected you in the storm, guided you, and blessed you.

What can you do during your times of trouble to RECALL the good?

• Meditate on His Word. God is the same yesterday, today and tomorrow.

• Read about the miracles He gave the heroes of the Bible.

• Remind yourself of all the things He has done in your life. Can't think of anything? Lawd! Let me help you out!

• He gives you the breath of life every morning.

• He encamps his angels around you as you go about your day.

• He's blessed you with family and loved ones, food, a job, shelter, transportation, and so much more.

• Remember where you were when you first came to the Lord. I'm sure you've changed a lot. Give Him glory for that!

• And if you don't know the Lord personally, just the fact that you are reading this book is proof that He is wooing you. He wants to have a relationship with you! Give Him praise for that!

• Don't make it all about you. Sometimes when you pray for others and minister to them, your problems don't seem as overwhelming. Psalm 105:5 CEB tells us "Remember the wondrous works that he has done, all his marvelous works, and the justice declared."

•

Yes, when I am low on funds I remember how He came through for me before...

1) When I didn't know how I was going to pay for my

dissertation edit #104, funds came from various places: consulting jobs, my sister-in-law Enid invested in me, some check came in the mail I wasn't expecting.

2) When I stopped working outside the home in 2007, my best friends loaned me some money. (Which of course I paid back!)

3)When I didn't have enough gas in the van or milk in the refrigerator, God worked through my secret sister program in my church, Save The Nations, to give me a card. "Just in time" coincidence? I think not!

God worked through the people in my life and recalling those instances reminds me of His goodness. What about you? What miracles has He worked in your life?

2) RESTORE

The second mind step is to restore our relationship with God and with others. Because of sin in our lives we need restoration for a number of things. We mess up with God *and* we mess up with others. The enemy lies to us and tells us that we can never recover from this or that all is lost. But God says this is not so. He can restore us. David prayed in Psalms 51:12 NLT, "Restore to me the joy of your salvation, and make me willing to obey you." David knew the damage that sin had done in his life. He knew that he needed restoration from the Lord. Sin had robbed him of his joy. Only the Lord could restore this joy to him.

Sin and failure among GOD'S people is nothing new; biblical history is littered with it. Samson failed. Abraham failed. Solomon failed. Jonah failed. The Hebrews failed. All twelve of the disciples of Jesus failed; even King David, who was a man after God's own heart failed; (2 Samuel 11:27 ASV). "But the thing that David had done displeased Jehovah."

So all of these people... committed willful, disobedient

sin, aiding and abetting the enemy *after having once pledged fidelity to GOD.* Does that sound familiar?

In both Testaments, the evidence of failure is overwhelming and sobering. So what does that tell us? That we're human! *But equally overwhelming is the evidence that GOD is in the restoration business.* Throughout the Word of God is the astonishing record of the Lord's effort to reclaim and to restore those who are eternally His, but who in a moment of weakness betrayed their initial allegiance. The potential for restoration plainly exists.

But in the biblical stories, not all who went astray were restored to the Body of Christ. What separates the restored from the doomed? **I believe it's four things**:

Honest and straightforward acknowledgement of failure. Restoration hinges on the honest and straightforward admission of the defiant soul's failure. Sin can never be addressed, if it is not named. It cannot be purged, if it is not identified. It cannot be cleansed, if it cannot be seen.

The second thing that separates the restored from the doomed is **Repentance.**

To repent is to change course, to reverse direction. Once confession has been made and forgiveness received, repentance must be demonstrated. An unmistakable commitment to turn away from the offending behavior must be made.

The third thing that separates the restored from the doomed is **Restitution.**

Some sins require restitution, the attempt to restore the loss someone else has suffered by our hand. Restitution typically involves a formal apology to the injured party and *evidence* of the offender's intent to repent. Reconciliation is always to be the stated goal and motive for this type of confrontation. The spiritual intent is to "gain thy brother or sister," not to lose them.

In my own life after my marriage crisis, the person(s)

involved — the woman, the friends who promised me not to gossip about it and did, etc. — none of them ever asked me for forgiveness. I always thought this is one of the most overlooked components of this very important process.

The final thing that separates the restored from the doomed is **Restorative Closure.**

When honest and straightforward confession has been made, repentance has been acknowledged and demonstrated, restitution has been pursued and completed, and a structure of loving discipline has been enforced, a formal end to the process should be recognized by the church body and/or its leadership. The memory of the sin should be sealed and removed from all conversation, and a celebration of the Lord's goodness and mercy should be enjoyed. The wounded soldier, now healed and repaired, should take his or her place back in the LORD'S service, free of the past and empowered spiritually to face the future.

When we come to our senses as did the prodigal in Luke 15, we, by the grace of GOD and HIS restorative process, can step back into the purposes for which HE originally created us. We can fight dependably, once more on the LORD'S side.

3) RECLAIM

The third step to prepare your mind for new belief systems is to reclaim your brain (you can't retrain it unless you reclaim it for God), which will then help you reclaim other things necessary for you to always have bounce-ability no matter what happens in life. Satan has done a lot of work on your brain to make you buy lies that have skewed your belief systems so you need to reclaim areas for God.

What are those areas? Well, you need to reclaim identity. You need to reclaim God's original purpose for your life. You need to reclaim God's promises for your life. Your inheritance, your place in the kingdom, your role in the greatest story ever told!

When we reclaim something, we bring it back from a negative condition.

So how is it exactly that we reclaim our brain?

•

"Our life is what our thoughts make it." — Marcus Aurelius

•

As we have been discussing throughout this book, our belief systems are rooted in our minds and the battlefield is the mind. The mind is the gateway to our heart. Whoever possesses it, possesses our heart! The transformation of our lives comes from the renewing of our minds. Our minds are the place that we evaluate those thoughts — aka belief systems — entering our heart. Look what the Word says about this:

Romans 12:2 NIV states:

Do not conform any longer to the pattern of this world, but be transformed by the renewing of your mind. Then you will be able to test and approve what God's will is — his good, pleasing, and perfect will.

Transformation means getting our mind changed!

In Romans 7:23-24 (NKJV) we see Paul stating, "But I see another law in my members, warring against the law of my mind, and bringing me into captivity to the law of sin which is in my members. O wretched man that I am! Who will deliver me from this body of death? I thank God — through Jesus Christ our Lord! So then, with the mind I myself serve the law of God, but with the flesh the law of sin."

When Paul says, "O wretched man that I am!" he does not imply a false humility that some men possess. I also don't think he is suggesting that God looks on him as a useless and horrible person despite his feelings of wretchedness!

What this passage does seem to suggest is that Paul is aware of his fallen nature and the war that goes on between his flesh and the spirit within (we often try to fake it).

Paul also points out an important factor in serving God and this factor has to do with his mind. He was aware of our need to *renew our minds*. I believe Paul was able to serve God faithfully because he had his mind spiritually renewed regularly.

•

For years I just said or did whatever came to my mind. Even though I was a Christian who loved God and attended church on Sundays, I had no idea that there was a battle going on in my mind. Nor had I heard that what I think, based on my belief systems as I've shared in this book, was very important to the outcome of my life. So... if I woke up in the morning and thought, I'm depressed, then I spent all day depressed. I hadn't learned that if I woke up with a thought that did not agree with God's Word, I could disagree with it and say, "No, this thought is a lie from the enemy."

Why is reclaiming the brain important? Our actions follow our thinking and our life outcomes depend on our actions! Our belief systems lay out the path for our life and destiny hangs in the balance. You haven't made progress in your path to destiny because your belief systems are all out of whack! You need to reclaim your brain! The first actions toward reclaiming our brain are to:

A) Come Into Agreement

Amos 3:3 asks how can two walk together unless they get into agreement? This verse tells us if we want to walk with God and see His good plan for our lives, then we need to be in *agreement with His Word*. But if we want to keep walking with the enemy and see his plan fulfilled in our lives, then all we have to do is just continue to agree with the miserable thoughts that he puts into our minds. But

I tell you this, your life won't change. The old cliché says the definition of insanity is doing the same thing over and over again expecting different results. Well if you don't align your belief systems with God's Word and expect your life to change, you're crazy.

In Genesis 3, as we have already discussed at length, the Bible tells us that Eve was deceived by the lies of Satan. It's pretty simple: Satan lied to Eve, she believed his lie, and she entered into sin convincing her husband to sin with her. And the world's been in turmoil ever since.

B) Take Responsibility

One of the things I hear from woman a lot as a pastor and as a conference speaker is that there is always a person (s) they blame. Now let me say that many times, the blame is justified. Perhaps those people really were evil! BUT, they are not living your life, YOU are, and while they are doing fine not even thinking about you, YOU have stopped living because you haven't taken responsibility for *your* response to *their* action. They were responsible for "their" actions toward you (let God get 'em) but you are responsible for your own actions! Because Eve lost the battle in her mind, life is now a mess for people who don't know the truth of God's Word. And if you don't learn to take responsibility, your actions will hurt those around you as well as yourself. Maybe not in a tangible way but simply because you will have never lived out your purpose; removing from the world the gift that was your life. Had I continued to believe all the lies the enemy told me, had I stopped trusting God in the midst of my situations and not looked to change my ungodly BS to godly BS, you wouldn't even be reading this book! This was part of my destiny but I would have forfeited that because I continued to believe a lie instead of God's truth.

First Corinthians 3:18-20 (The Message) says, "Don't fool yourself. Don't think that you can be wise merely by being up-to-date with the times. Be God's fool — that's the path to true wisdom. What the world calls smart, God calls stupid. It's written in Scripture. He exposes the chicanery of the chic. The Master sees through the smokescreens of the know-it-alls."

C) Don't Be A Know-It-All — Seek The Truth and Nothing but the Truth

I want to encourage you not to be a know-it-all kind of person. Resist being the type of person who thinks that you're always right and that no one else can teach you anything. I know a few people like that, perhaps you do too. It drives me crazy! Many of them are multi-gifted people, amazingly knowledgeable about the Word and other things but their know-it-all attitude keeps them from their destiny. When I run into those kinds of people, it takes everything in me not to run in the opposite direction. You know I have to be politically correct because well... I'm a pastor! But one thing I do make sure I do is not hang out too much with those people.

It just takes too much of my own energy to stand in the presence of these people because it's never a mutual exchange. They just know it all and want you to know how much they know.

•

Pride is a very dangerous thing and actually the sin that caused Satan to fall from the original glorious position that he had with God. Remember, he said, "I will exalt my throne above the stars of God... I will make myself like the Most High..." and I will, I will, I will! And God cast him down from that high place and he ended up not being anything that he thought he was going to be (Isaiah 14:12-15 NIV). Now he goes around trying to fill everyone's mind full of those same prideful thoughts.

There is a direct correlation between the quality of

your thoughts and the quality of your life. What you think determines who you are; it determines what you are; where you go; what you acquire; where you live; whom you love; where you work; what you accomplish.

4) RENEW

The fourth mind step is to renew your passion for the one and only God. You won't be able to change your belief systems and be motivated to keep believing for God's best in your life, if you don't renew your purpose from God and all this can't be done if you don't renew your mind as **Romans 12:2 NIV reminds us** "Do not conform any longer to the pattern of this world, but be transformed by the renewing of your mind. Then you will be able to test and approve what God's will is — his good, pleasing and perfect will."

Perhaps a definition would help.

Definition of Renew:

• Regenerate: reestablish on a new, usually improved, basis or make new or like new

• To make new again; to restore to freshness, perfection, or vigor; to give new life to; to rejuvenate; to reestablish; to recreate; to rebuild

This mind-step is just as important as the prior three. I don't know about you but in my marriage I need to keep the fire going. I have a weekly date night for that very purpose. My husband and I try not to let anything break that date. I mean anything. I have been married 22 years and I can truly say I love that man more today than the day I walked down the aisle. So I ask myself, can I say that about God?

You need to renew your passion for God! Many of us have allowed ourselves to lose our first love.

1. When my delight in the Lord is no longer as great as my delight in someone else, *I have lost my first love.*

2. When my soul does not long for times of rich fellowship in God's Word or in prayer, *I have lost my first love.*

3. When my thoughts during leisure moments do not reflect upon the Lord, *I have lost my first love.*

4. When I claim to be "only human" and easily give in to those things I know displease the Lord, *I have lost my first love.*

5. When I do not willingly and cheerfully give to God's work or to the needs of others, *I have lost my first love.*

6. When I cease to treat every Christian brother/sister as I would the Lord, *I have lost my first love.*

7. When I view the commands of Christ as restrictions to my happiness rather than expressions of His love, *I have lost my first love.*

8. When I inwardly strive for the acclaim of this world rather than the approval of the Lord, *I have lost my first love.*

9. When I fail to make Christ or His words known because I fear rejection, *I have lost my first love.*

10. When I refuse to give up an activity which I know is offending a weaker sister, *I have lost my first love.*

11. When I become complacent to sinful conditions around me, *I have lost my first love.*

God's greatest commandment, found in Deuteronomy 6:4-5, is to love our God with all of our being. It goes without saying that we cannot love someone we do not know. Get to know God and what He has done for you.

To grow in love with God, one needs to get to know Him.

Follow Jesus' example of praying constantly and consistently. When we examine the life of Jesus as well as that of Daniel and others who had a passion for God, we find that prayer was a vital ingredient in their relationships with God (even a quick reading of the gospels and the Book of Daniel reveals this). As with Bible study, prayer — sincere and open communication with God — is essential.

You cannot imagine a man and woman growing in love without communicating, so prayer cannot be neglected without expecting one's love for God to grow cold. Prayer is part of the armor against our greatest enemies (Ephesians 6:18).

We may have a desire to love God, but we will fail in our walk without prayer (Matthew 26:41).

Eliminate the competition.

Jesus said it is impossible to have two masters (Matthew 6:24). We are tempted to love the world (those things which please our eyes, make us feel good about ourselves, and gratify our fleshly desires) (1 John 2:15-17). James says that to seek to embrace the world and its friendship is hostility (hatred) toward God and spiritual adultery (James 4:4). We need to get rid of those things in our lives (friends who would lead us the wrong way, things that take up our time and energy and keep us from serving God more fully, pursuit of popularity, pursuit of possessions, and the pursuit of physical and emotional gratifications).

God promises that if we pursue Him, He will not only provide for our needs (Matthew 6:33) but will give us our desires as well (Psalm 37:4-5). If you know you are straying, begin to do what helped you grow in love with God in the first place.

It is not uncommon to have dips in a relationship. Peter dipped in his (Luke 22:54), and David dipped in his (2 Samuel 11), but they got up and pursued God once again. John, in Revelation 2:4, states it is not a case of "losing" one's love but "leaving" one's love. The cure is to do the "first works," those things that caused one to grow in love with God in the first place.

So my sistah, we need to renew our passion for God. Our first love awaits!

What were some of those things that caused you to fall in love with God? Go ahead, take out some paper and a pen and write down some of things you can do to fall in love again with the lover of your soul.

5) REMAIN

The fifth mind step that prepares you for Godly belief systems and the power to pursue God's best life for you is to REMAIN.

When you remain, you are determined to fulfill your personal destiny no matter what has happened in your past. Determined because God is just as determined to respond to you. "Determined in purpose and relentless in following through, you see everything that men and women do and respond appropriately to the way they live, to the things they do" Jeremiah 32:19.

John 15:1-10 states: "I am the true vine, and my Father is the vinedresser. Every branch in me that does not bear fruit he takes away, and every branch that does bear fruit he prunes, that it may bear more fruit. Already you are clean because of the word that I have spoken to you. Abide in me, and I in you. As the branch cannot bear fruit by itself, unless it abides in the vine, neither can you, unless you abide in me. I am the vine; you are the branches. Whoever abides in me and I in him, he it is that bears much fruit, for apart from me you can do nothing. If anyone does not abide in me he is thrown away like a branch and withers; and the branches are gathered, thrown into the fire, and burned. If you abide in me, and my words abide in you, ask whatever you wish, and it will be done for you. By this my Father is glorified, that you bear much fruit and so prove to be my disciples. As the Father has loved me, so have I loved you. Abide in my love. If you keep my commandments, you will abide in my love, just as I have kept my Father's commandments and abide in his love."

There is one true Vine, that is Jesus Christ. Those attached to this Vine, who have a connected relationship to the Vine through obedience, will be branches that bear true fruit. Fruit here is talking about the fruit of the Spirit and fruit of the Gospel. Those who love the Lord and demonstrate that love by obeying His commands will exhibit the fruit of the Spirit in abundance in their lives, and will bear the fruit of multiplying the Kingdom of God through preaching the Gospel.

Those who remain in Christ will produce true fruit. But we must never forget that God does not force the branches to remain or "abide." That choice is left up to the individual. There will be branches that do not produce fruit because they do not remain and do not love the Lord enough to obey His commands. These branches will be gathered up and thrown in the fire — the fire of eternal judgment. I know some of us don't like to hear about hell, but ladies, my job is to speak truth.

Luke 6:43 NIV "No good tree bears bad fruit, nor does a bad tree bear good fruit." Romans 7:5 (NIV) "When we lived to please our bodies, those sinful desires were pulling at us all the time. We always wanted to do what the Law said not to do. Living that kind of life brings death."

What kind of life brings death? Gal. 5:19-23 NIV tells us: "The acts of the flesh are obvious: sexual immorality, impurity and debauchery; idolatry and witchcraft; hatred, discord, jealousy, fits of rage, selfish ambition, dissensions, factions and envy; drunkenness, orgies, and the like. I warn you, as I did before, that those who live like this will not inherit the kingdom of God. But the fruit of the Spirit is love, joy, peace, forbearance, kindness, goodness, faithfulness, gentleness and self-control. Against such things there is no law."

Now some of you may be asking what does remaining in the vine have to do with pursuing destiny after life's storms or changing my BS? Perhaps this illustration can help:

Recently, I ran across an article about the growth and care of apple trees. The article clearly gained my attention when the writer said that orchard owners will frequently "wound" the trees to produce more fruit. These owners will carefully prune the trees with what is called "clean, flesh wounds." The owners are attempting in this process to limit the growth of leaves and wood in the trees. In fact, there are some who refer to this overall process as the "dwarfing" of the tree. In Maine and New Hampshire, the apple orchard owners give careful attention to the growth of the trees. Generally, the trees which are the most productive are not the ones that are the most beautiful.

In fact, sometimes a tree will really take off and begin to grow tall and *outwardly will look very beautiful* but have no fruit. This is where the concerned owner will move out into his orchard and will drop a huge wounding blow to the tree. The tree suddenly turns attention *from growth to healing.* In the efforts at healing, the tree turns its efforts from wood to fruit. The orchard owner does not just randomly decide one day to walk out into the orchard and start cutting his trees. For an owner to do so would severely damage the potential yield that comes from the orchard. He carefully watches the seasons and will then go about this almost terrifying process of wounding his trees. Fall or winter pruning will bring much damage to the tree and some never recover if they are wounded at the wrong time.

The orchard owner will "wound" his trees immediately prior to the spring and summer because this is the time of the most productive growth in the cycle of the tree. The "wounds" of the tree will heal during the time of Nature's greatest and perhaps most tender touch of growth!   Much can be said about this in a spiritual sense. It may seem as if the trials and tribulations that come our way are unplanned and sudden in their onset but God, who takes our spiritual growth into careful consideration, is never out of sync with the timing that is necessary to our progress in His Kingdom. He will "wound" us just prior to the times of greatest spiritual growth.

It is foolish for us to shake our fist at God and deem His patterns as ill-timed and without rhyme or reason. Trust in the Lord... He knows what He's doing! In addition to having a careful eye toward the season, the orchard owner will also give careful regard to which branches he "wounds" on his trees. He follows the guidelines that other apple growers have found to be useful. Ultimately the orchard owner will cut away the majority of the branches of the tree that only reach vertically or toward the sun. They have discovered that the most productive limbs are those which grow horizontally or lateral to the main trunk. Furthermore, the wounding of the *tree reduces the competition among the other branches.*

The lower the number of branches that are present on the tree, the more that each branch can focus on fruit production. When we remain in Him, He is going to do His pruning or wounding work so that we are productive, fruitful, aren't worried about "competition," and don't have long-term disease that limits fruit production. If you don't choose to remain [In Him], you also choose to be unfruitful. It's that simple!

Life is, has or is going to hit you hard! You have to make a decision *beforehand* that you will keep going. That nothing will come between you and YOUR savior, YOUR destiny, YOUR purpose!

Determination gives you the resolve to keep going in spite of the roadblocks before you. Let me tell you about Ludwig van Beethoven. My son has a CD collection of famous pianists that tells you about their lives as well as introduces you to their music. One day I listened as they talked about him, and I was amazed. You see everybody recognizes that Ludwig van Beethoven was a musical genius. But few realize the adversity he had to overcome to achieve greatness. In his twenties, Beethoven began to lose his hearing. Because he couldn't feel the music as he once had due to his hearing, on one occasion he said his fingers became "thick." His hearing problems haunted him into the middle years of his life, but he kept it a guarded secret. By the time he reached his fifties, Beethoven was completely deaf. But he refused to give up. Did you read that? HE REFUSED TO GIVE UP. He was once overheard shouting at the top of his voice, *"I will take life by the throat!"* Many of his biographers believe the only reason Beethoven remained productive for so long as he did was because of his *determination.*

I'm determined to make it on this side of heaven! To rise up again and again no matter the life storms that I go through. I'm not saying it is easy but I'm determined. I hope you will be determined to do the same with yours. I'm determined because I know that I know that God loves me. I used to believe the enemy's lies that I was God's stepchild, remember. But I now know that only HE saved my marriage because this girl from the projects just wasn't going to "have that." God took ahold of me. I could have given up many times in my life (childhood, teenage years, adulthood, *this morning!*), but I was determined to believe there was something better for me not only on the other side of this life, but on this side of heaven.

We all should have determination to prove the devil the liar that he is. Let me share another story:

There were two armies... one twice as strong as the other. The commander of the larger army sent a solider to the other asking for surrender. The commander of the smaller army called up three men.

To the first he said... "Fall on your sword." The man immediately stuck the hilt of his sword into the earth and then impaled himself on his own sword.

To the second the commander said, "Thrust yourself through with your spear." The soldier immediately went to a nearby tree where he fixed his spear firmly, the butt end braced against the ground among the roots. He backed off a few steps and then ran and fell on his own spear, the point thrusting through his heart.

The commander then turned to a third soldier and said, "Run and leap off of that cliff." The solider looked over the edge of the cliff to see the small thread-like shape of a river far below.

The soldier came running and with a leap disappeared over the edge to be dashed on the rocks below. Finally the commander turned to the foreign soldier and said, "I have 10,000 men who without hesitation will die for me like that... tell your commander I *demand* his surrender."

The soldier hurried back to their camp begging their commander to quickly surrender.

That is the kind of dedication a Christian is to have for Jesus Christ. We are to walk without fainting... never consider giving up but continue with determination and courage in your attempt to accomplish His will.

Determination is what helps ordinary people survive under the most terrible circumstances and they become extraordinary because of it! Mother Theresa said, "Life is a promise; fulfill it." You won't be able to do that without determination!

6) REBOUND

The final mind step to becoming a person who can eradicate the lies of the enemy is to know that you are rebound-ready. If you have done all five steps, the choice is yours because you are now ready for a rebound! We are *supposed* to bounce back better! You have taken a look at your old negative BS and have committed to replace them with positive, Godly BS. You can surely get up again! All the lies have kept you down long enough, don't you think?

Psalm 36:6 (The Message) states "God's love is meteoric, his loyalty astronomic, His purpose titanic, his verdicts oceanic. Yet in his largeness nothing gets lost; Not a man, not a mouse, slips through the cracks."

Isn't it awesome that God doesn't miss a thing?! Set in your mind that the Godly will rise again! The choice is always yours whether you stay down or get back up. It's all linked to what you believe. Someone once asked Paul Harvey, the journalist and radio commentator, to reveal the secret of his success. This is what he said, "I get up when I fall down." That is what rebounding is all about... getting back up.

There is also a good metaphor in the rebounds we know in basketball which means to gain hold of the ball. I like this illustration for rebounding because you are taking hold of the ball (the ball of your life) and you are playing on your terms, back in your court!

You're taking it back from the devil! Without question, rebounding is the most underappreciated skill in the game of basketball. But that doesn't mean it has to be hardest to learn. Whether you play inside or out on the perimeter, whether you're talking about offense or defense, and whether you play in the WNBA, NBA, high school, or church league, rebounding wins games. Rebounding also wins at life.

If you don't rebound, you can lose the game. Top WNBA players say rebounding is more than athleticism (how long you've been a Christian), or height (your status or titles in the world). A good rebounder dominates the boards (the Word of God), focuses on every play (knows and discerns the schemes of the enemy and makes right decisions), and works hard to make it happen. A good rebounder does what a person who loves God does — spends time with Him, reads the Word, fellowships with people who will help her go higher. So are you doing all you can to be a great rebounder?

More than physical ability or jumping higher than

the opponent, it's a combination of: mental focus, fierce determination, a tireless drive to succeed, and experience! A few years ago, a pastor friend of mine turned me on to the movie she was going to use for a sermon illustration titled *Never Back Down.*

The movie as she had already told me had great spiritual implications so I rented it. If you saw it, you will understand (if you didn't, go get it!). But this is what I learned...

• Everyone has a fight. You are not alone.
• You control the outcome. That is your responsibility.
• And you need to change your position.

To rebound, you have to get over the woe-is-me mentality.

Rebound readiness is also about perspective

Perspective is about how we see something. It's something like what Coach John McKay of the University of Southern California said to his team after they had been humiliated 51-0 by Notre Dame. McKay came into the locker room and saw a group of beaten worn-out and thoroughly depressed young football players who were not accustomed to losing. He stood up on a bench and said, "Men, let's keep this in perspective. There are 800 million Chinese who don't even know this game was played."

Get the right perspective. When Goliath came against the Israelites, the soldiers all thought, "He's so big we can never kill him." David looked at the same giant and thought, "He's so big I can't miss."

That's perspective!

You can change the ungodly BS that has kept you from living the life God wants you to live. You can get up from whatever life storm you've gone through, if you remember that God doesn't miss a thing!

Remember what Psalm 36:6 (The Message) states "God's love is meteoric, his loyalty astronomic, His purpose titanic, his verdicts oceanic. Yet in his largeness nothing gets lost; Not a man, not a mouse, slips through the cracks."

You think he doesn't know what you've been through? *He does.*

• You think he accidentally let YOU slip through the cracks? *He hasn't.*

• The word is clear... *Not a man not a mouse slips through the cracks.*

The choice is always yours whether you stay down or get back up. You can rebound from every situation the devil has sent your way because God hasn't forgotten you. He hasn't deserted you.

We need to remember that you can reach your destiny by changing your belief systems as you keep going back to the Word. God has this love story going on and He speaks in every book. God is *all over* the Bible meeting the needs of His children, making Himself known.

From the beginning of the world to its end, there is no place you can look and not see Jesus. He is everywhere. He is everything. "He is before all things, and in Him all things hold together." (Colossians 1:17 NIV)

No matter what lies you have believed, no matter how long they have kept you from your destiny, today you can get back up, you can rebound but it takes your wholehearted commitment. You have to give your very best effort. We half-step with God. God wants us to give our hundred percent.

It may not be your sister's hundred percent, but it's yours and that is what you will need for your rebound. You'll be surprised what you can carry in life and still get back up! You need to believe that YOU CAN beat the devil!

Wholehearted determination will get you back up living with a new belief system. You still got something left in you.

Today you can rededicate your life to giving God your very best. Even if you've lived with lots of the enemy's lies. You don't have to any longer. Only your belief systems will keep you from having the right mindset to give God all you got, to determine to rise again no matter what. Your destiny is within reach if you practice these things. So, the question for you today is: Can God count of you to keep going? Can God count on you to believe His truth and not Satan's lies?

MAKE IT PERSONAL

1) Which mindset is the hardest for you to have?

2) Why?

3) What ritual can you create to help you rid yourself of old BS and replace them with Godly ones?

EXERCISE: While it's likely that you have developed some positive belief systems as a result of this book (I sure hope so!), it's also possible that some negative ones refuse to go away. What negative belief systems are you having a hard time letting go of or replacing, even after reading this book? Explain why it is hard to let them go and how they have affected your life.

_____

_____

_____

CHAPTER 12

DO OR DIE

As I was writing this final chapter to this book that has taken me years to write, I found myself struggling with BS again. Especially since the agent who had originally signed on to represent me dropped me when she changed agencies. I guess I don't blame her. I took five years after signing with her, to get this manuscript completed. I could have let that stop me. I didn't.

I also found myself battling the thoughts that "I didn't have enough time," "I am doing too much already," "nobody is going to read this anyway," and a whole onslaught of lies. You see, the enemy doesn't stop. Even when you know the power of the truth. He is unrelenting and you have to be just as insistent as he is.

I refused to let doubts keep me from pressing forward on this book. And I refused to let the enemy's lies stand in the way of the work I have been called to do for the Kingdom. I rose above the hurt of my marriage crisis, and allowed God to strengthen our marriage so that our union can be a testimony.

I accept God's love and enjoy being the mother God has called me to be to both of my very different boys.

And get this: I've even made peace with my home church, the one that was the source of so much heartache and pain when I was a teen. Now I'm connected to that church because my family members are the senior pastoral leaders! I have even gone to preach and teach there! I realized that not everyone at that church was to blame for what happened. I had spiritual friends and family there who believed in the potential inside of me. Not everyone there wanted to see me die in the wilderness. Not everyone there believed in the labels people had given me as a teen.

And look at me know. I've preached there! Isn't God just like that? God blessed me to share a message about belief systems. It's the message I share with you here:

If you don't decide *right now* to do something about your

belief systems so that you can fulfill your purpose here on earth, you will die just the way you are. In 2 Kings 7:3 NIV we find a story of four lepers and there is a lesson for all of us in it. Let's read it together:

³Now there were four men with leprosy at the entrance of the city gate. They said to each other, "Why stay here until we die? ⁴If we say, 'We'll go into the city' — the famine is there, and we will die. And if we stay here, we will die. So let's go over to the camp of the Arameans and surrender. If they spare us, we live; if they kill us, then we die."

⁵At dusk they got up and went to the camp of the Arameans. When they reached the edge of the camp, no one was there, ⁶for the Lord had caused the Arameans to hear the sound of chariots and horses and a great army, so that they said to one another, "Look, the king of Israel has hired the Hittite and Egyptian kings to attack us!" ⁷So they got up and fled in the dusk and abandoned their tents and their horses and donkeys. They left the camp as it was and ran for their lives.

⁸The men who had leprosy reached the edge of the camp, entered one of the tents and ate and drank. Then they took silver, gold and clothes, and went off and hid them. They returned and entered another tent and took some things from it and hid them also.

The lesson for all of us here from these four lepers is that God wants you to move forward and trust Him. Like the song, by J. Moss, "God's Got It" and He wants you to act like it. These lepers, knowing that all around them was death due to the famine in the land, considered their options and all of them pointed to dying but one option provided a "what if" and that option was to go and face the enemy. Worst case, they get killed, best case they are shown mercy. But their best case was not God's ultimate scenario as God had caused their enemy to leave the camp, leaving all the food and clothes behind. These lepers got what they couldn't even imagine all because they decided to take a chance on God and *do* rather than believe their present situation and wait to die.

I don't know what you have been through but I do know that Satan has lied to you. I know this because that is what he does as the father of lies. I know this because you have a treasure within you that the enemy never wants the world to see. You don't have to have a platform of thousands to be special, dear one. Even if the only people you ever share with are your family and friends, all those people are of the utmost importance to our good God.

I want to encourage you to move forward and do. Don't die in your present situation. Don't look back either at all the things that have been done to you. Don't get stuck believing the lies. Your life is about so much more than ungodly BS and the deceit of the devil.

God wants to do a new thing in you. He wants to change those ungodly belief systems and replace them with the truth of His word. But He's going to need you to get up and move forward — even if that direction looks the enemy in the face.

God does not want us to be backward-looking, going through life looking in the rear vision mirror. But we so often can't help ourselves. We remember the hurts of the past and the mistakes we made.

It's time now to look ahead and focus on what's before us. God wants us to rise up to our full potential in Him. He has called us to do mighty things. We have got to keep on moving forward. It's only in moving forward that we ever accomplish what God has called us too. We can't stay where we are because we will die there. Nor can we go backward because we will die there, too. The only direction we can go is forward. Yes, it will be hard — but it's the only way if we want to move on in God and grow and get every blessing that He has for us! Just like the lepers, you don't know what you will find on the road that leads forward until you get up and move in that direction.

Psalm 118:17 NIV I will not die, but live, and tell of the works of the LORD.

The father of lies set out from day one to destroy you and he started like he did with Eve, through lies. You may have fallen for many of them but today is a new day. Today you can rise up and move forward with a new determination to be everything that God has called you to be. You will not die in the past or in the present lies of the enemy; you will live in the truth of God's Word and one day you will tell the world the works, the Lord has done in your life.

I want to hear about it too! So let me know by writing to me at drliz@cefl.org. Until then, move forward! The past is the past. They call it that for a reason. Don't let ungodly BS stand in your way any longer. Don't let the past get in the way of you, your life, or your destiny. Just keep on moving forward to make the future the best you can make it. You have the tools now to never have to buy a lie anymore from Satan.

It's Do or Die time. I hope you choose "Do!"

EXERCISE: Go back to the previous exercise, where you wrote about one or more negative belief systems you are having a tough time changing. Read over your words again, about how these belief systems have affected your life. No doubt, they have caused you harm. You don't want to keep living like that, under the burden of negative belief systems that are causing you hurt, pain, and anguish. Visualize what your life would be like if you were able to replace those negative belief systems. Write about that new life here, and then pray over this for the next week. Ask God to bring into your life these positive blessings and the positive belief systems to help you create this life. Notice the changes after this week of prayer and focus. Write about that here, also. You have been empowered to create positive change and God loves you so much that He is working on your behalf to help make it happen!

_____

_____

_____

For Further Help

Safe People: How to Find Relationships That Are Good for You and Avoid Those That Aren't by Henry Cloud and John Townsend

Successful Women Think Differently: 9 Habits to Make You Happier, Healthier & More Resilient by Valorie Burton

Biblical Healing and Deliverance: A Guide to Experiencing Freedom from Sins of the Past, Destructive Beliefs, Emotional and Spiritual Pain, Curses and Oppression by Chester & Betsy Kylstra

Spiritual Autobiography: Discovering and Sharing Your Spiritual Story by Richard Peace

Connect

I'd love to hear from you. Drop me a line to let me know how reading this book affected you.

You can **invite** me to speak at your event or have me at your book club via Skype or conference call by emailing me at drliz@cefl.org.

If you'd like to **stay connected** with what Dr. Liz is doing for women, visit her at www.cefl.org.

If you want to **be friends**, friend her on Facebook under Elizabeth Rios.

To find out about this and other upcoming **books**, visit her new author website at elizabethrios.com.